To Roberta and Bill,
   May we each emulate
Abraham Lincoln's bright
example!

   ~Susan Grace Dittman

ABRAHAM LINCOLN'S SHINING STAR

ABRAHAM LINCOLN'S SHINING STAR

The Inspiring Story of Abraham Lincoln and Nebraska

SUSAN GRACE DITTMAN

★ This book is dedicated
to each person who will follow
Abraham Lincoln's "bright example." ★

PRESIDENT LINCOLN LOVED TO study the stars. As a boy in the woodlands of Kentucky and then Indiana, he and his family would gaze at the stars from their tree-encircled clearing. On more than one occasion Abe must have climbed a tree in the childish hope that, by peering through its upper branches, he could get a closer look at the stars. Did he wonder, "How many are there?" and "How do they shine?"

Abraham Lincoln's fascination with stars grew when, as an adult, he spent thirty years on or near the open prairie. There, the star-spangled night skies are spectacular. Indeed, at night the prairie seems to become a vast open air theater, where the grasses and wildflowers give a standing ovation, the insects buzz their applause, and the fireflies signal their delight at the starry display. How could he not have become enthralled by stars?

As Lincoln traveled through the prairie on the circuit, he sometimes gave his horse free rein while he lounged in the buggy and read a book about astronomy. He would then eagerly await the night sky, so he could verify what he had just studied. He once said that he would not rest when "handling a thought" until he had "bounded it north, and bounded it south, and bounded it east, and bounded it west." The fathomless night sky, however, defied his attempts to understand it completely. So the more he learned about stars, the more curious he became.

During his presidency, he enjoyed riding by horseback in the evening to the Naval Observatory. There, he could view the heavens through the most powerful telescope in the country. He must have peered at the celestial bodies with awe as he plied the astronomer with questions.

In his wildest dreams President Lincoln could not have imagined that a special star would be named in his honor. What a fitting tribute! He would have been both humbled and delighted to learn of the Lincoln star. Ever curious, he would have inquired about its exact position, so he could view it through the telescope.

How surprised Abraham Lincoln would have been to learn that his star is not in the sky—it is on today's map of the United States. The fifty stars on the U.S. map represent state capitals, and Nebraska's capital is the only one named Lincoln, in his honor. What a perfect location, because Abraham Lincoln's decisions as president influenced Nebraska more than any other state. The president would have been equally surprised to discover that his state capital star actually shines, and in an amazing, faith-filled way. "Please!" President Lincoln would likely have exclaimed with great anticipation. "Tell me its story."

★ ABRAHAM LINCOLN'S SHINING STAR 7

"It's a boy!" undoubtedly rang forth on February 12, 1809 in a simple cabin in the frontier state of Kentucky. There, Thomas and Nancy Lincoln welcomed their second child and named him Abraham. As tiny Abraham slept and nursed and grew, he was peacefully unaware that America was bursting with the excitement of bold exploration.

Back east in Washington City, President Thomas Jefferson was preparing to retire from office. Six years earlier, President Jefferson had purchased so much land from France that the United States had doubled in size. Americans knew little about this land that stretched from the Mississippi River to the summits of the Rocky Mountains. Immediately, President Jefferson dispatched Meriwether Lewis to explore "The Purchase." Lewis asked his friend, William Clark, to co-lead this expedition, named the "Corps of Discovery."

Lewis traveled to William Clark's hometown, located at the southern edge of the Indiana Territory, just across the river from the state of Kentucky. From there, they recruited their Corps of Discovery team members. News of the exciting expedition must have reached Kentuckian Thomas Lincoln, who lived about fifty miles south of Clark's hometown. A bachelor at that time, Thomas Lincoln may even have contemplated joining the exciting expedition. Soon, Lewis and Clark completed their team and the Corps of Discovery set off.

"[I shall offer to heaven] my constant prayers for the preservation of our republic and . . . its best principles which secure to all its citizens a perfect equality of rights."

—Thomas Jefferson
February, 1809

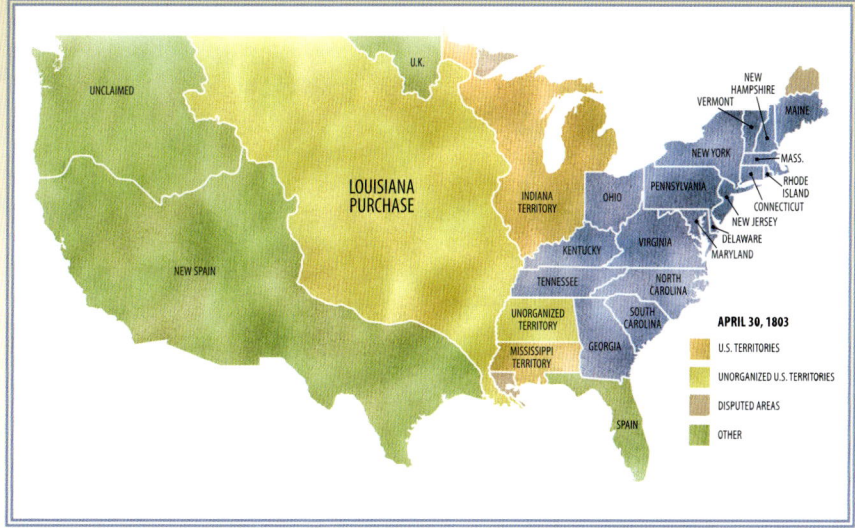

Upon reaching The Purchase, Lewis and Clark entered a giant prairie (*prairie* is the French word for "meadow"). This beautiful meadow swept from the Indiana Territory all the way west to the foothills of the Rocky Mountains. The explorers discovered that a land called *Nebrathka* lay at the center of the great prairie. *Nebrathka* is the Oto Tribe's word for "flat waters." Indeed, many shallow streams and rivers flow from the Continental Divide atop the Rocky Mountains through this prairie-adorned land. Eventually, this water flows into the Missouri River. One river is so wide and shallow that French trappers named it the *Platte*. In French this means—you guessed it!—*flat*.

As Lewis and Clark entered Nebrathka, they actually stood on bluffs that overlooked the Platte River Valley and the surrounding prairie. They admired the breathtaking view. They even made a short detour to explore the mouth of the Platte River before continuing along the Missouri River upstream to the Rocky Mountains.

Had the explorers ventured south of the Platte River, they might have explored the place that some day would become Abraham Lincoln's state capital star. Native Americans and trappers knew this place well. They often visited to gather the salt that lay there, salt which they then used to preserve their meat. Salt was plentiful because underground water frequently rose to the surface. This water contained salt crystals. In the hot prairie sun the water then dried, leaving behind streaks of salt. It was almost as if the ground cried salty tears of compassion at the sadness and cruelty that existed elsewhere on the earth.

When the Corps of Discovery finally returned triumphantly to Saint Louis in September of 1806, Thomas Lincoln had just married Nancy Hanks. Without doubt, the newlyweds would have heard about the completion of the voyage, since Lewis and Clark had journeyed through Kentucky on their way to Washington. The explorers passed within fifty miles of the Lincolns' log cabin. Perhaps Thomas and Nancy Lincoln even heard about the great meadow and the land called Nebrathka.

"Capt. Lewis and my Self walked in the Prarie on top of the Bluff and observed the most butiful prospects imaginable."

—WILLIAM CLARK, upon viewing the Platte River Valley

IN MID-FEBRUARY OF 1809 NANCY LINCOLN WAS BUSY caring for her newborn son as two-year-old Sarah insisted on offering her mama "help." At the same time, Meriwether Lewis was preparing to revisit Nebrathka and other lands they had explored. Later that year, however, Lewis died tragically. William Clark then became responsible for publishing their findings.

Meanwhile, Abe grew and learned to walk. From their dirt-floored log cabin, he and his family could watch a pioneer trail. In the days before radio or television, the activity on the trail entertained them immensely. Imagine Abe, wearing only a long shirt as toddlers did back then, watching pioneers and horses and covered wagons pass by. Sometimes slaves walked by, too. As little Abe grew a bit older, did he notice that these slaves looked sad and that some had chains on their wrists or ankles? Did any slaves smile kindly at the child who looked at them with such curious innocence?

When Abe was five years old, William Clark published two volumes that described the land of Nebrathka and other discoveries of their voyage. The Lincolns, of course, never saw these books. They were too poor to own any books, and neither Thomas nor Nancy could read. Meanwhile, the fascinating reports of the Corps of Discovery had fueled the pioneering spirit throughout America. And Thomas Lincoln caught this spirit of adventure.

A replica of Lincoln's boyhood home in Knob Creek, Kentucky.

"It [my early years] can all be condensed into a simple sentence ... 'the short and simple annals of the poor.'"

—ABRAHAM LINCOLN

THOMAS LINCOLN DECIDED TO MOVE HIS FAMILY to the new state of Indiana. He chose Indiana in part because, unlike Kentucky, it was a free state. That meant that slavery was outlawed within its borders. Indeed, Abe must have grown up hearing his parents and neighbors discussing the contentious issue of slavery.

Abe was almost eight years old when his family moved to the Indiana wilderness. It was a frightening time for him. Years later, he wrote this poem:

> *When first my father settled here,*
> *'Twas then the frontier line:*
> *The panther's scream filled night with fear*
> *And bear preyed on the swine.*

When Abe was just nine years old, his mother died. Thomas Lincoln soon left for Kentucky, leaving Abe and his sister Sarah alone. How Abe and Sarah must have cried and cried salty tears. Perhaps the Bible stories and hymns their mother had taught the children helped to comfort them. As Abe endured this heartache and challenge, he was developing great courage.

Three difficult months later, Thomas Lincoln returned with a stepmother for Sarah and Abe. Abe's new stepmother brought several books with her and Abe treasured these books. The Bible taught him to know and to do what is right. The biography of George Washington inspired him to love America.

"We reached our new home about the time the State came into the Union. It was a wild region with many bears and other wild animals still in the woods. There I grew up."

—ABRAHAM LINCOLN

Early Indiana settlers called the cougars "panthers."

"[My] father and family settled a new place ... at the junction of the timberland and prairie ... [where we] fenced and broke ground."

—ABRAHAM LINCOLN

ABE WORKED HARD IN HIS FAMILY'S FIELDS, AND HIS father often hired him out to work for neighbors. Abe then gave all of his hard-earned wages to his father to help their family. This was common back then. Did this prompt him, as he worked long days in the fields, to imagine what life must be like as a slave? Sometimes, as he worked in the warm sunshine, he must have tried to remember the face of his mother. Perhaps this made him think of slave children who were often separated deliberately from their parents. Did he shiver with horror at this thought?

As a young man, Abe earned extra money for his family when he transported cargo upon a flatboat down the Mississippi River. (He would later make a second flatboat trip.) When he ventured into the Deep South, he witnessed firsthand the cruelty of slavery. Years later he described this disturbing experience: "That sight [of chained slaves] was a continued torment to me ... and continually exercises the power of making me miserable."

In 1830 the Lincolns moved to Illinois. Thomas chose farmland where the forest met the prairie. With his father Abe dug into the strong, thick roots of the prairie plants. They also lifted and removed many heavy rocks to clear the land. At the end of a hard day of work, when the setting sun painted the sky in a glorious way, Abe must have looked westward and marveled at the beauty of the world. He may also have wondered what lands lay beyond the sunset.

Advertisement for slaves in Washington City, or Washington, D.C.

"Slavery is founded in the selfishness of man's nature."

—ABRAHAM LINCOLN

Slave pen near Washington, D.C.

When his family moved again, Abe was an adult and he chose to stay behind. Abe worked at different jobs and, in 1834, campaigned successfully for a seat in the Illinois General Assembly. He studied hard to become a lawyer and now preferred to use his full name, Abraham. In time he began to court a woman named Mary Todd. They both knew a proud politician from Illinois named Stephen Douglas, who may also have courted Mary Todd.

On November 4, 1842, Mary Todd married her "tall Kentuckian." Abraham and Mary eventually had four children, nicknamed Bob, Eddie, Willie, and Tad. They also had a dog named "Fido" and a horse named "Old Bob." (Their horse wasn't old, but they didn't want to confuse him with their son named Bob.)

Lincoln served eight years as a state legislator. Interestingly, when states were brand new, towns competed fiercely for the prize of becoming the new state's capital city. In the Illinois state capital of Vandalia, Abraham Lincoln was pleased to capture this prize for his hometown of Springfield. Ever since, Springfield has been the state capital of Illinois.

In 1846 Abraham was elected to the U.S. House of Representatives. This required him to spend two years in Washington. At that time our nation's capital was a main center for the slave trade. Representative Lincoln must have walked past slave pens and slave auctions in and near Washington. Did he cry with compassion at the heartbreaking scenes of black people being sold into slavery?

Lincoln bravely began to fight for what is right. He proposed a bill to eliminate slavery in the nation's capital. Slave owners, however, convinced the city officials of Washington to oppose Abraham Lincoln's bill. Their opposition doomed Representative Lincoln's effort. He also supported a colleague's bill to ban the trade of slaves in Washington, but this bill failed to pass.

"Let reverence for the laws be taught ... in schools, in seminaries, and in colleges."

—ABRAHAM LINCOLN

After he completed his two-year term in Congress, Abraham Lincoln returned to Springfield, Illinois. When Zachary Taylor ran for the U.S. presidency, Lincoln campaigned wholeheartedly for him. Lincoln hoped that if Taylor were elected, the new president would appoint him to a government job in Washington. Taylor did win, but seemed to forget all about Abraham Lincoln.

In 1849 (the same year as the California Gold Rush) he returned to his law practice. He earned most of his yearly income by working as a lawyer on the circuit court. This meant that twice each year he spent two or three months traveling in a big circle, or circuit. Sometimes he hitched Old Bob to a carriage; sometimes he rode Old Bob bareback. Together, they rode through the prairie towns of Illinois.

The prairie here could grow as tall as the withers of a horse. Indeed, tallgrass—or true—prairie once stretched from western Indiana all the way to the place that would become Lincoln's shining star. (Farther west, as rainfall diminishes, the prairie shrinks to mixed grasses before becoming shortgrass prairie.) Lincoln must have admired the exquisite sunsets over the tallgrass prairie, never dreaming that some day, out West, a state capital would be named in his honor.

Eventually, President Taylor contacted Abraham Lincoln, offering him the governorship of the large Oregon Territory. Lincoln declined the offer. He continued to practice law exclusively, both in Springfield and on the circuit court. His "retirement" from politics would prove to last six years.

"WE LOST OUR LITTLE BOY," ABRAHAM LINCOLN wrote in early 1850 upon three-year-old Eddie's death. "We miss him very much," he added, numbly. This tragedy prompted Abraham to move from doubting whether God really existed to an honest searching for God. That spring he rode on the circuit and grieved with the wildflower-blanketed prairie as his comforting friend. He began to read his Bible in earnest and realized that the Bible was what it claimed to be: the Word of God.

During Lincoln's six-year-long retirement from politics, approximately 200,000 pioneers followed the Platte River upstream to the Rocky Mountains and beyond. That was a lot of people following one river. Fortunately, the vast majority of these travelers headed in the same direction across the Nebrathka lands that were, by this time, commonly referred to as "Nebraska Country." Once across Nebraska Country, the pioneer traffic dispersed to Utah, Oregon, and California.

The one-way Platte River Highway, as it is often called, straddled both sides of the river. On the northern banks the so-called Mormon Trail ran the entire length of Nebraska. The Oregon Trail met up with the Platte River farther west and stayed on the river's southern banks. Nestled between these two famous pioneer trails lay the place that would some day become Abraham Lincoln's shining star.

"To read the Bible, as the word of God himself . . ."

—ABRAHAM LINCOLN

Officially, the U.S. Government had declared the land called Nebraska "Indian Country." This meant the land was permanently reserved for Native American Indians and was off-limits to white settlers. Thus, pioneers could not settle in the beautiful prairie that lay beside the Platte River Highway. The only white settlers allowed to live in Indian Country were Indian agents (the U.S. government's representatives to the tribes), U.S. soldiers, fur traders, and missionaries. In addition some whites (known as squatters) settled illegally in Indian Country. No one from these groups settled in the remote, uninhabited area that would become the Lincoln star.

"Resolve to be honest."
—Abraham Lincoln

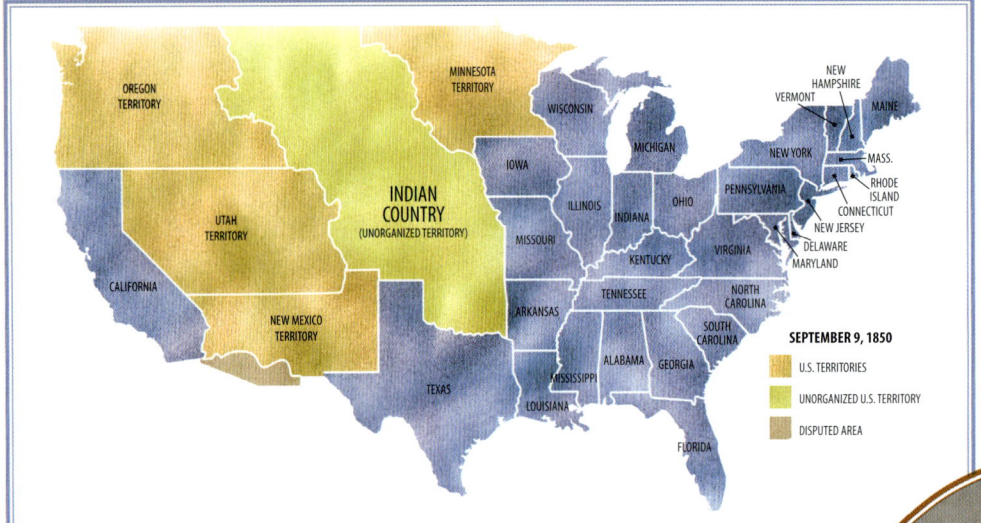

U.S. map in 1850 which shows the huge "Indian Country."

By this time Abraham and Mary Lincoln's acquaintance Stephen Douglas had become a U.S. senator and the chairman of the Senate's Committee on Territories. Thus, Douglas oversaw the process by which U.S.-owned lands became U.S. territories. It was a powerful position.

Tragically, Douglas did not think it was important to keep promises. For instance, he planned to break the U.S. government's twenty-year-old promise to Native American Indians. He would shrink the Indian Country into what is today the state of Oklahoma. To relocate these tribes, the government would have to renegotiate its treaties with them.

This would clear the way for him to organize a vast "Nebraska Territory." Perhaps he wanted to create a safe central pathway for a transcontinental railroad. A Chicago-anchored northern route through this proposed territory, rather than a southern route, would benefit his home state of Illinois. Perhaps he wanted to develop the land between the East and the West so that states would stretch from coast to coast. Whatever his reason, with determination he championed the creation of a Nebraska territory.

Senator Douglas was nicknamed the "Little Giant" because of his short stature and his political power.

> "Our reliance is in the love of liberty which God has planted in our bosoms."
>
> —ABRAHAM LINCOLN

Meanwhile, Abraham Lincoln continued to practice law. As he increasingly read anti-slavery publications, his hatred of slavery grew. On the open prairie, Lincoln must have searched the star-spangled night skies for the North Star. Did he wonder how many slaves at that very moment were following that very star in a daring quest for freedom?

He was comforted by his belief that slavery would be confined to the South and would slowly die out in the United States. Indeed, the Missouri Compromise restricted slavery in the land obtained through the Louisiana Purchase. This important compromise essentially prohibited slavery north of an imaginary line that was an extension of Missouri's southern border. It also set a precedent of political appeasement: for each free state Congress admitted, it simultaneously admitted a slave state. In this way Congress maintained the balance of power between the "anti-" and "pro-" slavery factions.

As the United States prepared to absorb vast new lands, the political struggle over slavery became even more problematic. Continuing the policy of appeasement, Stephen Douglas helped to broker an additional compromise in 1850. This compromise tragically included a harsh Fugitive Slave Act. With its enactment slave catchers invaded the North to return runaway slaves to their masters. (Lincoln reluctantly maintained that northern states legally had to enforce this act.) "Runaways" now had to follow the North Star all the way to Canada to find safety. As Lincoln gazed at the shining North Star, perhaps he was inspired by how it boldly and steadfastly served as a beacon for freedom.

At last Senator Douglas was able to answer the Nebraska question. In December of 1853 a bill was introduced in the Senate to organize the former Indian Country into a new Nebraska Territory. Under the thirty-year-old Missouri Compromise, slavery would be prohibited in this new territory. For this reason, Southern legislators protested the Nebraska Bill. The Senate then sent the measure to Douglas's Committee on Territories.

There, in a series of steps, Douglas drastically revised the Nebraska bill. His decision to create a second new territory (Kansas) aroused little controversy. To win Southern support for the bill, however, he audaciously planned to give both new territories "popular sovereignty." This meant the settlers themselves would vote to determine whether their territory would enter the Union as a slave or a free state. Until this vote took place, slavery would be legal in the two territories. But this contradicted the Missouri Compromise, which prohibited slavery in this region. So that popular sovereignty could take effect, Stephen Douglas revised the Nebraska Bill to repeal the Missouri Compromise. Outcry in the North spread like a racing prairie fire that, according to one pioneer, "crackle[d] like musketry."

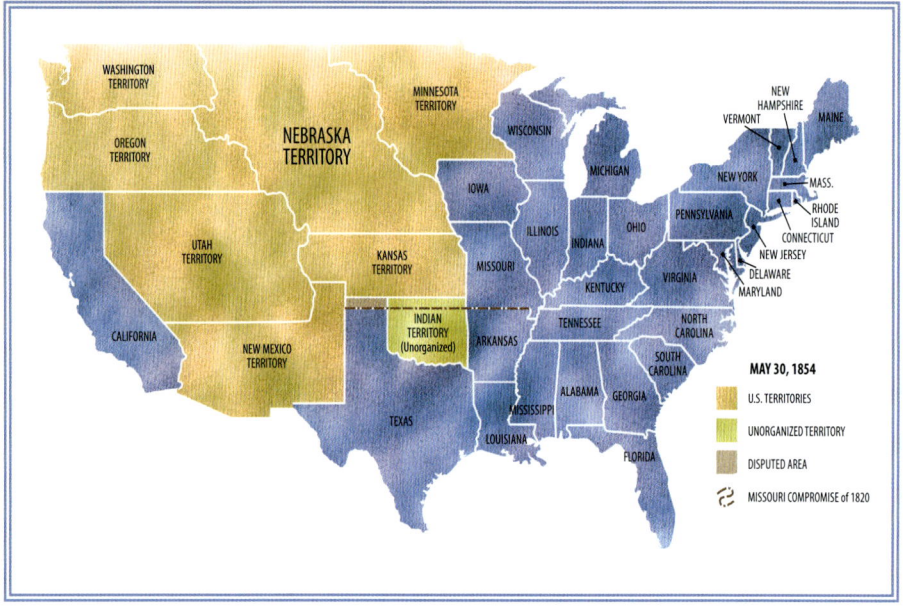

States and territories of the United States on May 30, 1854.

Abraham Lincoln was "thunderstruck and stunned" when he learned of these developments. He realized that, if the Nebraska Bill became law, for the first time slavery would be legalized in this land that stretched all the way to the northern border of the United States. Would Nebraska and Kansas vote to become slave states? Congress would eventually carve other, smaller territories from the vast Nebraska Territory. Would these new territories also have popular sovereignty and vote to become slave states?

Lincoln wondered if the Nebraska Bill was actually a conspiracy to spread slavery first in the West and then throughout the entire United States. He feared that slave states might gain a majority in Congress and force the entire United States to allow slavery. Abraham Lincoln spent more and more time pondering this bill. He later explained that he was roused as he had "never been before" when the Senate and the House of Representatives passed Douglas's version of the Nebraska Bill.

". . . the monstrous injustice of slavery itself."

—Abraham Lincoln

"I plainly see that you and I would differ about the Nebraska law. I look upon that enactment, not as a law, but as a violence from the beginning."

—ABRAHAM LINCOLN

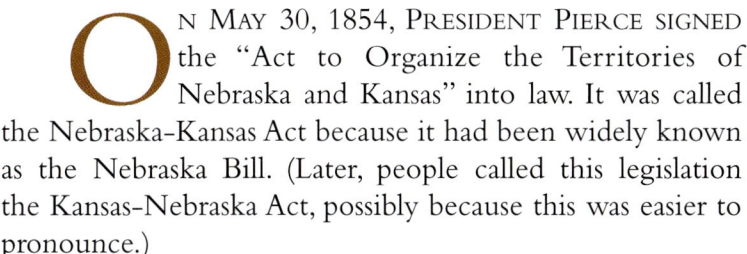

ON MAY 30, 1854, PRESIDENT PIERCE SIGNED the "Act to Organize the Territories of Nebraska and Kansas" into law. It was called the Nebraska-Kansas Act because it had been widely known as the Nebraska Bill. (Later, people called this legislation the Kansas-Nebraska Act, possibly because this was easier to pronounce.)

Perhaps all alone, beneath the star-filled night sky of the prairie, Abraham Lincoln promised to stand bravely for what is right. He started by going to the library. There he studied all he could about the Nebraska-Kansas Act and U.S. history. He prepared many arguments against what he called "the Nebraska law."

As white settlers entered the brand-new Nebraska and Kansas territories, Abraham Lincoln entered politics again. He began by giving speeches in support of a politician who had strongly opposed the Nebraska Bill and who was now campaigning against the Nebraska-Kansas Act. Soon, more and more people wanted to hear Lincoln speak. During this time, Senator Douglas toured Illinois to speak in support of the Nebraska-Kansas Act. Abraham Lincoln challenged him to a debate, but the senator refused. So when Douglas gave a speech, Lincoln spoke right afterwards.

"That is the issue that will continue in this country when these two tongues of Judge Douglas and myself shall be silent. It is the eternal struggle between these two principles—right and wrong—throughout the world."

—ABRAHAM LINCOLN

The crowd at one of the Lincoln-Douglas debates that took place in 1858.

TOP RIGHT: Abraham Lincoln's presidential running mate was Senator Hannibal Hamlin of Maine.

ABRAHAM LINCOLN RAN FOR ELECTION TO THE SENATE in 1855. When he lost that race, he returned to his law practice. Persevering, three years later he ran for Senator Douglas's own Senate seat. Douglas finally agreed to debate Abraham Lincoln. They debated at seven different locations and more than ten thousand people attended each event. Although Abraham Lincoln lost the Senate election, he gained national prominence for his eloquent speeches that stated clearly what is right.

In 1859 Abraham Lincoln actually came fairly close to the place that would become his shining star. He traveled to western Iowa and stood on bluffs that overlooked the Platte River Valley. Admiring its beauty, he remarked later that this would be the ideal path for a transcontinental railroad.

Abraham Lincoln then began to run for the office of president of the United States. Supporters, including Alvin Saunders whom he had met in Iowa, worked to ensure that their party chose Abraham Lincoln as its nominee. It did. In the national election three candidates ran against Lincoln, including Senator Stephen Douglas. When voting was completed, Abraham Lincoln had won. Fireworks and cannons exploded in his hometown of Springfield, Illinois.

Fido, the Lincolns' dog, was terrified of these noises. As the Lincoln family prepared to move to Washington, they realized that their dog would be frightened of the loud train ride and the big-city noises. With sadness, they left Fido with their neighbors. President-elect Lincoln decided to give the family's living room sofa to these neighbors, too. This way Fido could curl up on his favorite sofa and not miss them as much. Fido's new family promised the president-elect not to scold Fido if the dog came inside with muddy paws.

> "All should have an equal chance. This is the sentiment embodied in the Declaration of Independence. . . . I would rather be assassinated on this spot than surrender it."
> —ABRAHAM LINCOLN

ALMOST IMMEDIATELY upon Lincoln's election, Southern states began seceding from the Union. Lincoln determined to keep his promise to preserve the Union—even if it meant war. Recalling the Nebraska Bill that had roused him so profoundly, perhaps he was deeply encouraged in January of 1861 when he learned that the Nebraska Territory had voted to outlaw slavery within its borders.

As he left Springfield for Washington, he said to the crowd, "Trusting in Him [God] who can go with me, and remain with you, and be everywhere for good, let us confidently hope that all will yet be well." Abraham Lincoln's writings reveal that by this time he knew and relied on God. Throughout his presidency, his reliance on God grew progressively closer as he experienced God's presence and guidance.

Abraham Lincoln bravely risked his life to pursue his conviction that slaves should be free. On the way to his inauguration, he stopped at Independence Hall in Philadelphia. Near the Liberty Bell, and not far from where the Declaration of Independence was signed, he raised a flag and declared that he was willing to risk assassination for the principle of freedom for all. Right afterwards his aides learned of a well-planned assassination plot against him. Wearing a plain hat (instead of his trademark stovepipe hat) and hunched over to disguise his height, the president-elect had to sneak into Washington just before dawn.

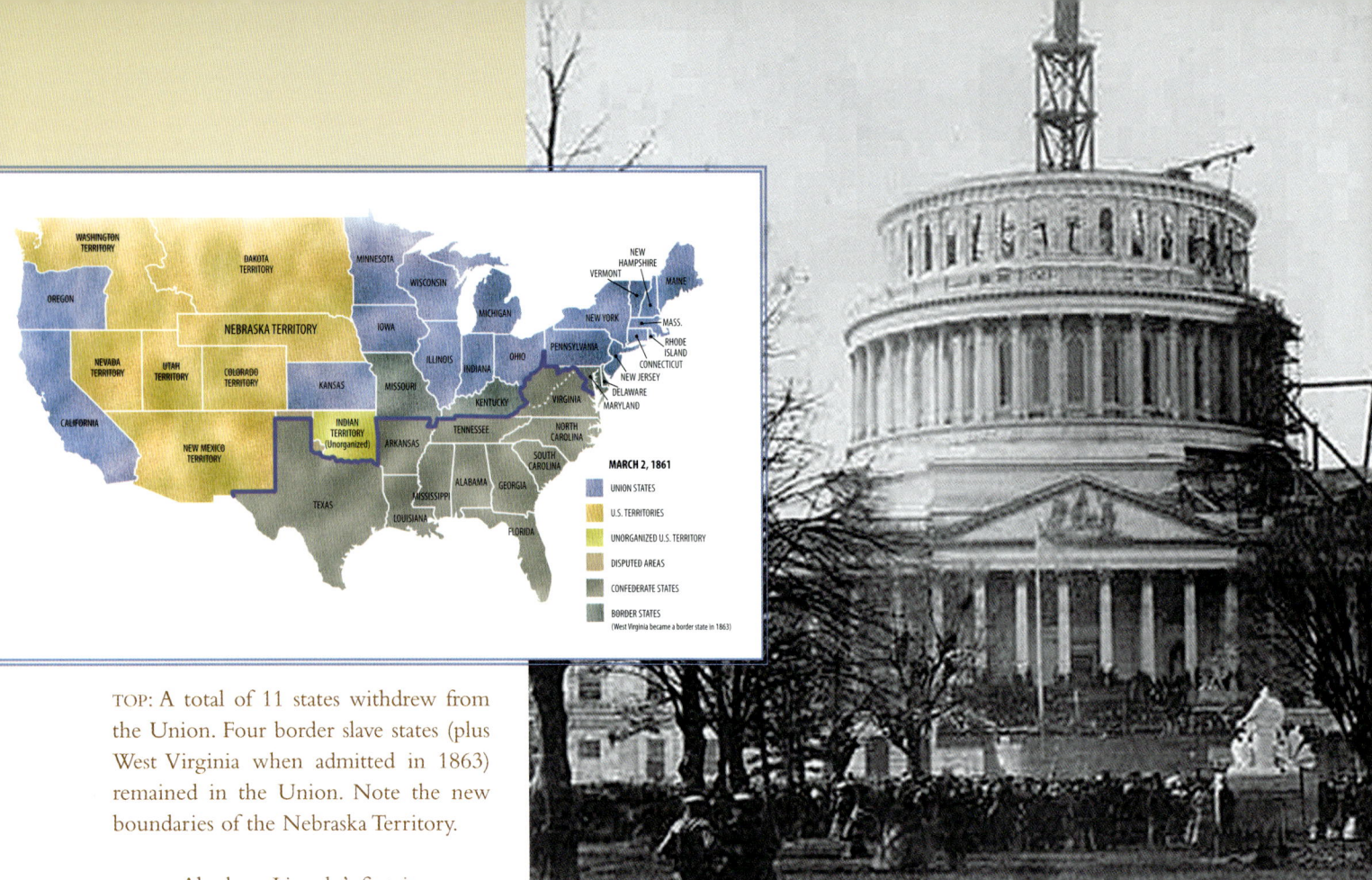

TOP: A total of 11 states withdrew from the Union. Four border slave states (plus West Virginia when admitted in 1863) remained in the Union. Note the new boundaries of the Nebraska Territory.

RIGHT: Abraham Lincoln's first inauguration on March 4, 1861.

"Plainly, the central idea of secession is the essence of anarchy."

—ABRAHAM LINCOLN
First Inaugural Address

TWO DAYS BEFORE LINCOLN'S INAUGURATION, outgoing President James Buchanan signed into law the legislation that created the Dakota Territory. Interestingly, Abraham Lincoln's brother-in-law was a key lobbyist for this legislation. This move reduced the once-vast Nebraska Territory to approximately one-fourth of its original size.

During Lincoln's inaugural ceremony, Senator Douglas sat in the very front row. Eyewitnesses said he noticed that President Lincoln, about to give his inaugural address, had no place to put his hat. In a beautiful gesture of humility, Douglas reportedly reached for President Lincoln's hat and held it during the entire speech.

Senator Douglas never meant for the Nebraska Bill he had championed to destroy the Union. He simply had not understood that slavery was evil. By the time Abraham Lincoln was sworn in as president of the United States, seven states had left the Union and formed the Confederate States of America. Senator Douglas met with Lincoln and promised to visit the border slave states to try to persuade them to remain loyal to the Union. This time Senator Douglas kept his promise. While on this important mission, Senator Douglas became ill and died soon afterwards.

When the Confederate States of America attacked Union-held Fort Sumter in South Carolina, the Civil War began. The Union flag atop that fort was lowered in defeat on April 14, 1861.

> "But for it [the Bible] we could not know right from wrong."
> —Abraham Lincoln

Already, a Union soldier had been killed in a military skirmish. President Lincoln was heartbroken. He had known this soldier well, and he held the young man's funeral in the White House. Soon the president called for volunteers, and the North responded. So did the sparsely populated Nebraska Territory. It raised the First Nebraska Regiment of 1,000 men and, later, a second regiment of cavalry. Abraham and Mary Lincoln deeply loved all the soldiers who fought and risked their lives for the Union. These soldiers became known as "Abe Lincoln's Boys in Blue."

There were so many desperate times during the Civil War. President Lincoln said that his "own wisdom was insufficient for the day." He asked God for wisdom and read his Bible often, sometimes several times a day. Abraham Lincoln quoted the Bible more often in his speeches than any other president. He said that the Bible is a great gift from God and is the only way we can know right from wrong. He met with many devout leaders, including Sojourner Truth and Frederick Douglass. Surprisingly, President Lincoln never used the word "enemy" to describe Confederate soldiers or ordinary citizens. He considered them simply to be his fellow Americans.

When President Lincoln was weary, he sometimes enjoyed a refreshing game of tag with children, whom he called his "little friends." Lincoln must have been quite the sight, racing about on the White House lawn with his coattails flapping behind. Some people said this was unbecoming for a president, but Lincoln loved playing with children. President Lincoln also read joke books to help him laugh during times of great sorrow. When his schedule allowed, he loved to go to the Naval Observatory to study stars through its powerful telescope. He needed breaks like this from his heavy burdens.

> "I made a solemn vow before God that if General Lee were driven back from Maryland, I would crown the result by the declaration of freedom to the slaves."
>
> —Abraham Lincoln

One and a half years after the Civil War began, President Lincoln decided to emancipate the slaves. It was the right thing to do. But how could he accomplish this? Lincoln believed that he would not violate the U.S. Constitution if he freed slaves by issuing a military edict in time of war. So he drafted an edict that he named the Emancipation Proclamation. As a military measure, it could only apply to the Southern states that were fighting against the Union. (It could not apply to border slave states, for these remained in the Union.) To free slaves permanently in the entire United States, the U.S. Constitution would have to be amended.

The Emancipation Proclamation would make it clear that the Civil War was no longer simply about preserving the unity of the United States. The Proclamation would proclaim that the war was also a fight to free the slaves. Therefore, a Union victory would be a triumph over the evil of slavery. A Union victory would both free the slaves in the South and prevent slavery from spreading to the western U.S. territories.

When Lincoln presented his draft of the Emancipation Proclamation to his cabinet officials, the war was not going well for the North. Confederate General Robert E. Lee was invading the nearby border state of Maryland and was threatening to invade Washington. President Lincoln's cabinet urged him to wait until the Union had won a battle. The president listened to their advice and locked the document in his desk drawer. Then, all alone, he prayed to Almighty God. He asked God to drive back General Lee from Maryland and promised that, when this happened, he would announce the Emancipation Proclamation to the world.

ABRAHAM LINCOLN'S SHINING STAR

"On the first day of January, in the year of our Lord one thousand eight hundred and sixty-three, all persons held as slaves within any State or designated part of a State, the people whereof shall then be in rebellion against the United States, shall be then, thenceforward, and forever free . . ."

January 1, 1863

"Whatever shall appear to be God's will, I will do."
—ABRAHAM LINCOLN

SEVEN WEEKS LATER, LINCOLN'S PRAYER WAS ANSWERED in a stunning way. General Lee sent his military plan for the upcoming battle to his field commander. Because this field commander liked to smoke cigars, General Lee cleverly wrapped his battle plan around a gift of three cigars. A careless Confederate courier, however, dropped this package in a large field where a Union soldier somehow discovered it. Imagine the shock of this Boy in Blue when he realized what he held in his hands.

Thanks to this military intelligence, the Union won the terrible Battle of Antietam and drove General Lee out of Maryland. True to his promise, Lincoln announced the draft of his Emancipation Proclamation. The president then signed it into law on January 1, 1863.

> "The probability that we may fail in the struggle ought not to deter us from the support of a cause we believe to be just."
>
> —ABRAHAM LINCOLN

THE VERY NEXT DAY—THAT'S RIGHT, THE VERY NEXT day—Abraham Lincoln's capital star officially began to take shape. On January 2, 1863, Captain William Donovan filed the first homestead claim on remote land that would someday become part of Lincoln's shining state capital star. Captain Donovan named the surrounding area Lancaster in honor of his hometown in Pennsylvania. As a former steamboat captain, he had come west to seek his fortune—in salt. Salt was still in great demand as a meat preservative, so money could be made gathering and selling it. Captain Donovan began building his salt factory, which he anticipated would be quite profitable.

Soon Reverend John Young arrived. Reverend Young filed his homestead claim in the very place that would be at the heart of Lincoln, Nebraska—Abraham Lincoln's shining star. He declared that he had three goals:

1. He dreamed of building a Christian seminary for women. Because there were so few women in the entire Nebraska Territory, this seemed impossible.

Saltgrass grows on the edges of the saline patches that can still be found in Lancaster County.

2. He dreamed of starting a village that would become the county seat. Even the idea of starting a village, much less its future as a county seat, seemed ludicrous. The inhabitants of this wild area were coyotes and buffalo—not people!

3. He dreamed that this village would become a state capital. This third goal was simply preposterous.

Reverend Young named this settlement Lancaster Village. He boldly prepared a map that was twelve blocks long by eight blocks wide. Of course, he named the central road "Main Street." He named the road right beside it "Lincoln Street" in honor of his President, whom he loved and admired.

He and several pioneers who had accompanied him went to work building their cabins. Next, Reverend Young began to build the seminary. His first dream was coming true.

Meanwhile, President Lincoln was preparing to travel to Gettysburg to dedicate a cemetery. (During the Civil War, new cemeteries were often built and dedicated, because so many Americans were killed.) His son Willie had died the previous year, and now Tad was ill. Nevertheless, the president was determined to speak where thousands of Boys in Blue had sacrificed their lives for the cause of freedom.

As he prepared to write his speech, Lincoln's thoughts must have turned to Psalm 90. This is the only psalm that Moses wrote in the Bible. Indeed, slaves often referred to Lincoln as their Moses because Moses had led more than a million slaves to freedom. In the tenth verse of this Psalm, Moses wrote, "The days of our years are threescore years and ten; and if by reason of strength they be fourscore years . . ." (KJV).

In his speech, President Lincoln wanted to avoid mentioning the U.S. Constitution because it had not yet been amended to give equality to all men. Instead, he traced our nation's beginning to the issuance of the Declaration of Independence in 1776. The difference between 1863 and 1776 is 87 years, or "four score and seven years."

He began to write his speech:

> *Four score and seven years ago our fathers brought forth on this continent a new nation, conceived in liberty, and dedicated to the proposition that all men are created equal.*

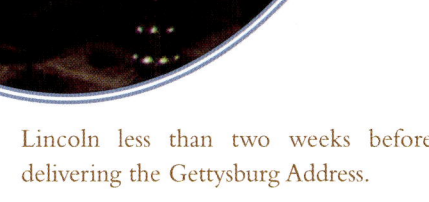

Lincoln less than two weeks before delivering the Gettysburg Address.

President Lincoln traveled to Gettysburg to give his brief address. Some people liked it; many did not. But Abraham Lincoln had spoken what he knew to be right. On the return trip he and his aide fell ill with smallpox. The aide died, but President Lincoln's case proved to be milder. After the president had regained his strength, he began to work mightily to persuade Congress to pass the Thirteenth Amendment to the U.S. Constitution, which would permanently ban slavery in America. Following his passionate year-long effort, Congress finally passed the amendment. President Lincoln had succeeded! It would now be up to the states to ratify the Thirteenth Amendment to the U.S. Constitution.

"That we here highly resolve that these dead shall not have died in vain . . ."

—Abraham Lincoln
Gettysburg Address

We return him to you [Illinois] a mighty conqueror.
Not thine anymore, but the nation's; not ours,
but the world's.
Give him place, O ye prairies."

—Pastor Henry Ward Beecher,
on the assassination of Abraham Lincoln

The lowering of the Union flag at Fort Sumter on April 14, 1861, had marked the start of the Civil War. Exactly four years later—on April 14, 1865—the Union flag was raised over Fort Sumter in victory. Finally, a long and bloody Civil War was coming to a close.

That very night an assassin shot President Lincoln.

President Lincoln lingered near death for nine hours, as his close friends and colleagues gathered around his bedside. As he was taking his last breaths, his pastor and good friend Reverend Phineas Gurley said, "Let us pray." Every man knelt near the bed and prayed. Soon afterwards, President Lincoln died.

The nation—North and South—wept salty tears of sorrow. At the White House, Reverend Gurley eulogized the slain president. Then a train carried Abraham Lincoln's body to Illinois. The train stopped along the way so that Americans could pay their respects to their beloved president. In Philadelphia, city officials remembered the words Abraham Lincoln had spoken so bravely at Independence Hall. They positioned his open casket so that his head was close to the Liberty Bell.

In Springfield, Illinois, a riderless Old Bob walked behind the carriage that carried his master's coffin. The funeral procession made its way to the cemetery where Abraham Lincoln's body was placed in a receiving vault. The prairie that he so loved lay nearby. From the heights of Lincoln's burial place, visitors can still watch the sun set in a glorious blaze over the very western land that ignited his passion to defend liberty for all.

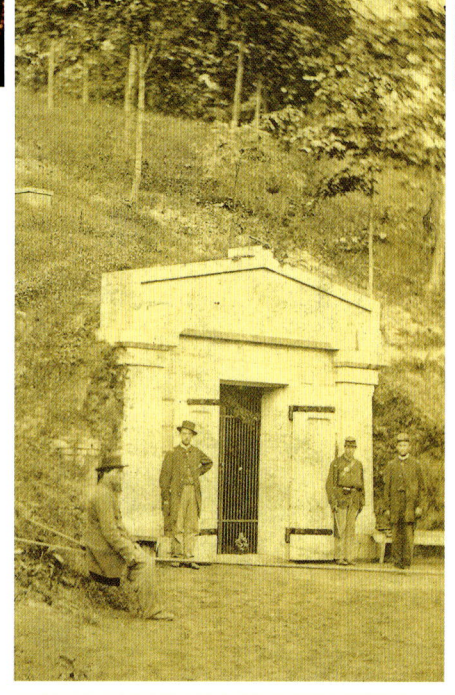

Lincoln's Boys in Blue guard the receiving vault at Oak Ridge Cemetery where Lincoln's casket was placed in its temporary resting place.

The Nebraska Territory had greatly influenced Abraham Lincoln's political career. Now, Abraham Lincoln's decisions as president guided the formation and growth of the Nebraska Territory. Indeed, no one did more to influence the development of Nebraska than Abraham Lincoln. In fact, Abraham Lincoln would influence Nebraska more than any other state!

Following Lincoln's death, several colleagues discovered a document on his desk. Soon after he became president, Lincoln had remembered Iowan Alvin Saunders's loyalty and had appointed him the territorial governor of the Nebraska Territory. Saunders was now up for reappointment, and President Lincoln had actually signed the certificate to authorize this. Apparently, one of Abraham Lincoln's last official acts as president was to designate the person who would guide the transition of the Nebraska Territory into statehood.

With the war over, a bittersweet air of excitement filled the territory. Yes, the Nebraska Territory would finally become a state! President Lincoln himself had signed the Nebraska Enabling Act which invited this territory to apply for statehood in the Union. Now, as Nebraskans were about to reap the benefits of the initiatives that President Lincoln had signed into law, statehood appeared imminent.

Indeed, it was President Lincoln who had authorized the Morrill Land Grant Act. This meant that states would receive public land from the federal government for the creation of colleges, especially to further the study of agriculture. This act transformed society because now the common person could obtain a college education. Thanks to this legislation, Abraham Lincoln's legacy would include the soon-to-be-created University of Nebraska.

President Lincoln, with his appreciation of farming, had also created the Department of Agriculture. How appropriate that the future state of Nebraska would play a leading agricultural role in the United States and would thus benefit greatly from the programs of Lincoln's agency. Several Nebraskans would even serve as secretary of the Department of Agriculture.

"That this nation, under God, shall have a new birth of freedom, and that government of the people, by the people, for the people, shall not perish from the earth."
—Abraham Lincoln
Gettysburg Address

Like Lincoln, Territorial Governor Alvin Saunders was born in Kentucky. He lived near Springfield, Illinois, for several years.

In neighborly fashion, homesteaders would often team up to plow. Many homesteaders, however, could not afford to buy horses, oxen, or mules, so they hand-plowed the land.

> "Every man should have the means and opportunity of benefitting his condition."
> —ABRAHAM LINCOLN, advocating the Homestead Act

President Lincoln had signed into law two momentous pieces of legislation—the Homestead Act and the Pacific Railroad Act—that were now transforming the West, including the Nebraska Territory. These two laws would impact the future state of Nebraska more than any other state.

Lincoln had signed the Homestead Act to promote settlement of the West by citizens of the Union, as well as to promulgate agriculture. This act granted up to 160 acres of free public land to the settler who laid claim to it. After paying a small filing fee, the homesteader had to live on the claim for five years and improve the land. Alternatively, he or she could live on the claim for just six months, then purchase it for two hundred dollars. Ultimately, this act would give away approximately 10 percent of the land area of the contiguous United States.

Compared with today's states, the future state of Nebraska would have the highest percentage of land distributed under this act. Indeed, almost half—45 percent—of Nebraska's land would be claimed successfully as homesteads. North Dakota would be second with 39 percent, and approximately one-third of Montana, Oklahoma, Colorado, and South Dakota would be successfully homesteaded.

In the Nebraska Territory, Daniel Freeman had filed what reportedly was the first homestead claim. A Boy in Blue, he convinced the district land office to open at 12:01 A.M. on January 1, 1863, which was the day the homestead law went into effect. That way, he could file his claim and still report to Fort Riley, Kansas, later that day. Eventually, the gracious decision on the part of that land office registrar would lead Congress to locate in Beatrice, Nebraska, the one and only national park that commemorates the Homestead Act.

This boy is "breaking sod" as Lincoln did in his boyhood. Homesteaders were required to cultivate ten acres. Plowing ten acres was equivalent to walking one hundred miles.

Women homesteaders in the Sandhills gather "cow chips" for fuel. Approximately one-tenth of total homestead claims in Nebraska were filed by women, who "proved up," or earned, their claims as successfully as men.

In October of 1866, Union Pacific Railroad executives celebrated reaching the 100th Meridian, which was approximately 250 miles west of Omaha. Feeder lines were expected to connect here with the transcontinental railroad.

THE TRANSCONTINENTAL RAILROAD WAS A MIND-BOGgling engineering feat that would truly unite the western "colonies" with the East. President Lincoln, who was an expert in railroad law, had himself chosen its central route. This meant that the Union Pacific had begun construction in Omaha. Working westward, the Union Pacific would lay track all the way across the Nebraska Territory. This railroad company would eventually link up with the Central Pacific, which had begun its work in Sacramento, California. Between Nebraska and California, the transcontinental railroad would pass through today's states of Colorado, Wyoming, Utah, and Nevada. The legislation that Abraham Lincoln had signed would impact Nebraska significantly more than these other states, for two reasons.

First, President Lincoln had authorized not only the transcontinental railroad but also several feeder lines that would join the main line in Nebraska. These feeder lines would ensure that the transcontinental railroad would be well connected to other parts of the country. The federal government was issuing land to the two main railroad companies—as well as to the feeder railroad companies specified in the legislation—to fund railroad construction. These land grants would represent approximately 16 percent of Nebraska's total acreage today. This percentage would be roughly double that of each of the two runners-up: present-day Nevada and Wyoming.

Second, more of these land grants would be subdivided and sold to settlers in the future state of Nebraska than in any other host state. That's because the land grants in Nebraska were fertile and suitable for farming or ranching. Elsewhere, the land was arid or mountainous. Not only was Nebraska's land fertile but the "iron highway" would enable Nebraska farmers and ranchers to ship their products to distant markets. As a result, this act would entice thousands of Americans and Europeans to settle in the Nebraska Territory. Permanent towns would spring up all along these new rails in Nebraska.

"He from whom all blessings flow must not be forgotten."
—ABRAHAM LINCOLN

> "Their conduct was splendid. They alone repelled the charge."
>
> —GENERAL LEW WALLACE, describing the First Nebraska Volunteer Infantry

BY THE END OF THE CIVIL WAR, MORE THAN A THIRD OF the enlistment-eligible men in the Nebraska Territory had served as Lincoln's Boys in Blue. This was quite a respectable contribution of manpower. Now these men began coming home from the war.

The Nebraska men who returned to their homes first were those who had enlisted with Union regiments in other states. Most commonly, these soldiers had signed up with regiments in Missouri, Illinois, Iowa, and Kansas. Most of the Nebraska men, however, had responded to the federal government's call for soldiers by enlisting with the First Nebraska Volunteer Infantry. The conclusion of the Civil War found this regiment still engaged in battle, albeit as a cavalry unit in the so-called Indian War.

The First Nebraska Volunteer Infantry had formed in the summer of 1861 in Omaha. Soon afterwards, the volunteers embarked for Missouri under the leadership of Nebraskan Colonel John Thayer. In Missouri, they engaged in a few skirmishes. It wasn't until early 1862 that they saw real action. At that time, they joined up with General U.S. Grant's Army of West Tennessee.

In February of 1862, the First Nebraska played a pivotal role in the Battle of Fort Donelson, in Tennessee. There, they fought under General Lew Wallace's command. (Lew Wallace was from Indiana and would gain fame after the war as the author of the bestselling *Ben-Hur—a Tale of the Christ*.) Following this battle, General Wallace commended the Nebraskans by saying, "They met the storm, no man flinching, and their fire was terrible. To say they did well is not enough. Their conduct was splendid. They alone repelled the charge." Church bells rang throughout the North at the news of this important victory. President Lincoln promoted Grant to major general, and Grant, having shown no leniency to the vanquished general, earned his famous nickname, "Unconditional Surrender."

A scene from the battle of Fort Donelson

In April of 1862, Nebraska soldiers again fought with distinction. This time it was at the costly Battle of Shiloh, also in Tennessee, in which they helped drive back the Confederate Army. (Ironically, *shiloh* means "peace.")

After these two major battles, the First Nebraska Volunteer Infantry spent the summer in Tennessee and Arkansas. By the fall of 1862 the regiment had returned to Missouri. That winter was especially difficult, as the Nebraska soldiers endured starvation and deprivation. They even left bloodstained footprints as they marched in the snow, because some men were barefoot.

In October 1863, while still in Missouri, the regiment was converted to a cavalry unit. Officially, it became the First Nebraska Veteran Cavalry. Its mounted soldiers served mainly in Arkansas, where they frequently skirmished with small Confederate units.

In August 1864, the First Nebraska Volunteer Cavalry was sent to help defend Nebraska against Native American Indian attacks. The Sioux and Cheyenne were attacking settlers and travelers in Nebraska. They were also attacking the transcontinental telegraph and the stagecoach stations along the Platte River Valley. To aid in the Indian War, two invaluable companies were formed: the Omaha Scouts and the Pawnee Scouts. The Omaha and Pawnee Scouts fought heroically to help quell the uprising.

In 1866, the volunteers were finally discharged and replaced by regular soldiers of the U.S. Army. The Native American Indian Scouts and—at long last—the men of the First Nebraska Cavalry could return to their homes. Seven percent of the soldiers of the First Nebraska never came home, however, having died in battle or from disease or accident.

Two Medals of Honor were awarded to Nebraska soldiers during this period. One was awarded to Francis Lohnes of the First Nebraska Veteran Cavalry for gallantry in defending government property during the Indian War. The other was given to Victor Vifquain, a bonafide swashbuckler who had emigrated from Belgium to the Nebraska Territory. Vifquain signed up with a French-speaking New York regiment that was eventually dissolved because of widespread insubordination. After an independent foray into Confederate Territory as part of a fantastic plot to kidnap Confederate President Jefferson Davis, Vifquain signed up with the Ninety-seventh Illinois Infantry. He earned his Medal of Honor at the close of the war by capturing a Confederate flag at the Battle of Fort Blakely, in Alabama. In an incredible coincidence, he was ordered to capture the fleeing Confederate president. Vifquain succeeded in commandeering the train that was supposed to be carrying Jefferson Davis, but Davis was not on it.

"It has pleased Almighty God to vouchsafe signal victories..."
—Abraham Lincoln
Thanksgiving Proclamation after victories at Fort Donelson and Shiloh

Colonel Robert Furnas and his staff of the Second Nebraska Cavalry. This unit was formed in 1862 to fight the Sioux who had massacred white settlers in Minnesota and then escaped west. The Second Nebraska disbanded a year later.

As homesteaders settled far from tree-lined rivers and streams, they built houses of sod.

"Write me a long yarn [story] about something to amuse me."

—Abraham Lincoln

Because the war was over and in large part because Abraham Lincoln's policies were under way, the population of the Nebraska Territory began to swell. Thousands of Union veterans from other states streamed into the territory. Settlers also were arriving from other states, as well as other countries. In addition, many newly freed African Americans came to homestead in this territory. Other freed slaves came, not to homestead but to find work as cowhands, cavalrymen, railroad laborers, or meat packers.

In the sparsely treed prairie, settlers began to build houses called "soddies." Soddies were made using bricks of sod. This sod was brick-like because prairie grasses developed thick, deep root systems to survive both strong winds and periods of drought. With a wit that Abraham Lincoln would have enjoyed, they nicknamed these sod bricks "prairie marble."

Abraham Lincoln, who had loved a good joke, would have chuckled at the pranks that the prairie played on the settlers. A cow might graze on the roof of a soddie that was dug into a hill. More commonly, while the inhabitants of soddies ate their meals or slept in their beds, critters like snakes would dangle from the sod ceiling and drop in on them.

"With malice toward none; with charity for all; with firmness in the right, as God gives us to see the right . . . to do all which may achieve and cherish a just and a lasting peace amongst ourselves and with all nations."

—ABRAHAM LINCOLN
  Second Inaugural Address

By the time the Nebraska Territory began to apply for statehood, Congress had reduced the territory's size even further so that it was approximately the same size as today. With these new boundaries, the Platte River divided the Nebraska Territory almost in half geographically. The two sides of the Platte were bitter political rivals.

The "North-Platters" had the territorial capital of Omaha, whereas the "South-Platters" had the greater population. This population advantage should have meant a voting majority in the territory's legislature. North-Platters, however, regularly rigged the population count so that the North actually enjoyed the voting majority. This made the South-Platters fighting mad. The feud was so bitter that sometimes shouting matches (and even fistfights with brandished guns and knives) erupted in the legislature. South-Platters, however, finally gained their rightful majority in the legislature.

To make matters worse, North-Platters and South-Platters needed to cooperate to apply for statehood. In 1866 they submitted a state constitution that restricted voting rights to "free white males." (At that time, most state constitutions contained this discriminatory clause.) Congress passed a bill to approve Nebraska's application. President Andrew Johnson, battling Congress, pocket-vetoed the measure. The next year Congress again approved Nebraska's application, but this time with a condition. The Nebraska legislature had to remove the words "free white" from its state constitution and provide assurance that it would not deny the right to vote (or any other right) to black males. President Johnson vetoed this congressional measure, but Congress overrode his veto. Abraham Lincoln would have been very disappointed by this sad chapter in Nebraska's history.

A print depicting one of several raucous scenes in the territorial capitol in Omaha.

The Great Seal of Nebraska bears the state's motto: Equality Before the Law.

Once the Nebraska legislature agreed to change its state constitution as Congress had stipulated, statehood became official. When the Nebraska legislature notified President Johnson of its compliance, the president proclaimed Nebraska's statehood. This occurred on March 1, 1867, which is considered the state's birthday. At long last, Congress could revise the U.S. map to include the thirty-seventh state. A problem, however, remained. On the map, the brand-new state lacked a star. Its legislators needed to agree on a location for their state's capital.

Would Nebraska's capital be located north of the Platte River, in the former territorial capital of Omaha? Or would it be moved somewhere south of the Platte? Both sides of the Platte fought to have the capital city prize. It was like a mini-civil war, albeit this time without fistfights. With statehood, the legislature was maturing.

Desperate to defeat a bill that would locate the new state capital south of the Platte, a North-Platter—from Douglas County—proposed naming the new state capital "Lincoln." Perhaps he hoped that a few South-Platte legislators who had bitterly opposed President Lincoln's policies during the Civil War would then vote against this bill. As the story goes, one influential South-Platter instantly leaped onto his desk. Intent on capturing the state capital prize, he enthusiastically accepted this suggestion. Thus, the new capital—to be named Lincoln—would be located somewhere south of the Platte River. It took some time for North-Platters to adjust to this sudden decision of placing the state capital in "southern" Nebraska.

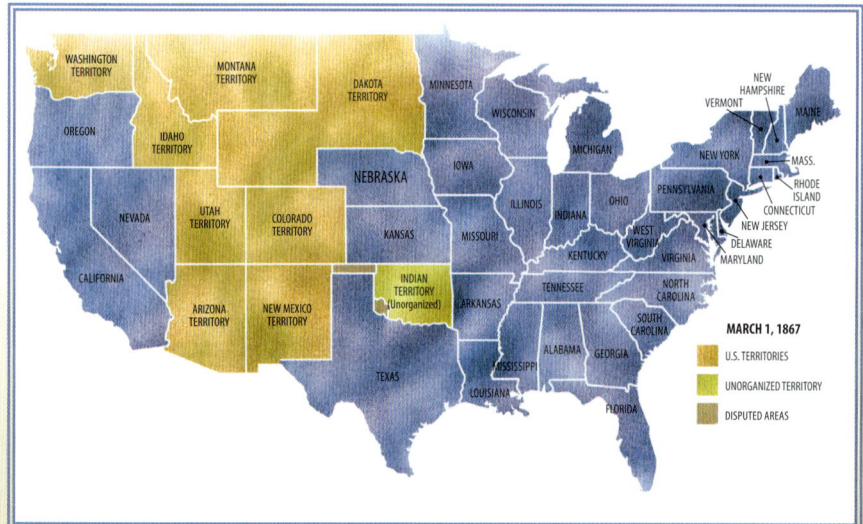

States and territories on March 1, 1867.

"In locating a town, select a large wet prairie or field, full of bogs and springs; so much so, that it will bear to be called Swamp-field, Spring-field, or the like."

—Vandalia newspaper, when Abraham Lincoln succeeded in "removing" the Illinois state capital from Vandalia to Springfield

The earliest photograph of downtown Lancaster Village, taken in 1868.

Nebraska's first state capitol, built in 1868. The building would eventually crumble because of defective blocks of limestone.

Which town south of the Platte River would become the new state's capital? Three towns competed for this tremendous honor. Nebraska lawmakers agreed to form the Nebraska State Capital Commission to solve the predicament. The Commission visited the first town (Ashland), but found too many mosquitoes. They visited the second town (Yankee Hill), but decided that its residents had tried to bribe them by extravagantly serving ice cream. They then visited the third town of Lancaster Village, a town so tiny that it had only about thirty residents. Captain Donovan showed off its then-promising salt industry. Reverend Young offered to donate the seminary lands if they selected the Village. (Sadly, the seminary had operated for only three years when a fire destroyed the building.)

In the end, the Commission decided that Lancaster Village was "just right." Against all odds, Reverend Young's third daring dream came true. Lancaster Village won! It became Lincoln, the brand-new state capital of Nebraska. At long last the one and only Lincoln star could be placed on the map of the United States.

> "I say 'try.' If we never try, we shall never succeed."
> —Abraham Lincoln

Lincoln's Boys in Blue became government leaders in the new state and worked to finalize Nebraska's counties. When possible, they named Nebraska counties to honor Abraham Lincoln. During the Civil War, territory leaders had removed the county names of four men who were linked to the Confederacy. They renamed these counties for Lincoln-appointee Governor Alvin Saunders, for Lincoln's cabinet members William Seward and Edwin Stanton, and for Abraham Lincoln himself. Interestingly, the territory leaders left the name of Douglas County unchanged. (It is likely that Stephen Douglas had influenced the original decision to name this county for himself.) Maybe, just maybe, they recalled that Stephen Douglas had kept his promise to Abraham Lincoln.

Nebraska Boys in Blue continued this naming tradition for the next twenty years or so, as settlement moved westward within the state. They named many new counties for Civil War leaders. Generals Grant, Hayes, Garfield, and Arthur were also selected as county names after they became U.S. presidents. Lincoln's Boys named other counties for American statesmen and government officials whom Abraham Lincoln had appreciated.

Meanwhile, the region named Lancaster had become Lancaster County. And Lancaster Village had become the county seat of this county, fulfilling Reverend Young's second dream. Now that Lancaster Village had been chosen as the state capital, all three of Reverend Young's daring dreams had come true. Officials, however, needed to designate the renamed village of Lincoln as the new county seat. They honored Abraham Lincoln by doing this on February 12, 1869. This date marked the sixtieth anniversary of Abraham Lincoln's birth.

ABRAHAM LINCOLN'S SHINING STAR

At long last Abraham Lincoln's star was in place. It was ready to shine. But how can a state capital star actually shine? Reverend Phineas Gurley showed the way when he spoke at Abraham Lincoln's funeral. Beside the body of our beloved president, Reverend Gurley challenged all Americans with these words that ring through the ages: "to emulate your [Lincoln's] bright example will be the truest mark of our respect, the best tribute we can offer."

That's it! Even now, in the twenty-first century, that's how Abraham Lincoln's state capital star shines. Abraham Lincoln set a "bright example." As Nebraskans follow his glowing example, the Lincoln star shines. The more Nebraskans who do this, the brighter the illumination.

Of course, the shine of Abraham Lincoln's "bright example" is not confined to Nebraska. As people throughout the Midwest, and even throughout America, emulate Abraham Lincoln's way of living, his radiant legacy will beam there, too. The more Americans join in, the greater the radiance.

> "To emulate your [Abraham Lincoln's] bright example will be the truest mark of our respect, the best tribute we can offer."
> —Reverend Phineas Gurley,
> at Abraham Lincoln's funeral

Does it seem impossible to follow such a "bright example"? Begin by promising, with determination, to emulate Abraham Lincoln as best you can. It is inspiring to remember that President Lincoln promised to preserve the Union and kept his promise despite seemingly insurmountable difficulties.

The next step is to understand Abraham Lincoln's great character, for this is what made his life worthy of our admiration. Reverend Gurley, who knew Lincoln very well, said at Lincoln's funeral, "Always and everywhere he [Abraham Lincoln] aimed and endeavored to be right and to do right." Reverend Gurley explained Lincoln's other excellent character traits. Most of these character traits can be summed up in one word: love.

Reverend Gurley went on to explain the secret of Abraham Lincoln's great character:

> *But more sublime than any or all of these [character traits], more holy and influential, more beautiful and strong and sustaining, was his abiding confidence in God, and in the final triumph of truth and righteousness, through Him, and for His sake. This was his [Abraham Lincoln's] noblest virtue, his grandest principle; the secret, alike of his strength, his patience, and his success.*

While it may seem impossible to live like this, be encouraged by the following stories of Nebraskans who have done so.

> "I turn and look to the great American people and to that God who has never forsaken them."
> —ABRAHAM LINCOLN

"Thou shalt love the Lord thy God with all thy heart, and with all thy soul, and with all thy mind."

—Matthew 22:37 (KJV),
quoted by Abraham Lincoln

Reverend John Young founded and mapped Lancaster Village.

Do you remember Reverend John Young who founded Lancaster Village, which later became the state capital city named Lincoln, Nebraska? He loved his country and grieved mightily when President Lincoln died. At the same time, how excited he was that the war was over. He could finally welcome home his son. His son had served in the Civil War, undoubtedly as one of Abraham Lincoln's Boys in Blue.

When struggling pioneers arrived, a friend observed that Reverend Young was "always ready with words of cheer and a little cash, when needed. He would always find some work for those willing to work. He would manage somehow to make work for them." The friend continued, "He loved to make money for the sole purpose of doing good with it. Place a mountain of gold at his door and he could not be rich while anyone was in need or there was a laudable enterprise to help."

Reverend Young, like Abraham Lincoln, read the Bible often and knew it well. He believed it was right to serve others with humility and love. Whether it meant facing winter storms or camping out at night, "where any good was to be accomplished no task was too hard for him." His friend concluded, "Among the useful and good, he [Reverend Young] was among the best." In his largely unnoticed way, Reverend Young followed Abraham Lincoln's "bright example."

OTHER NEBRASKANS' STORIES BEGAN TO UNFOLD JUST twelve years after Lincoln's death. A brave Indian chief, an army general, a newspaper reporter, and a judge in Nebraska worked together to help rescue Native Americans from terrible oppression in the United States. Interestingly, they did this in Douglas County, Nebraska.

In 1877 the U.S. government forced the Ponca tribe to leave its homeland in Nebraska. They had to march on foot to Indian Country in present-day Oklahoma. The journey was named the "Ponca Trail of Tears" because so many tribal members died along the way and upon arrival. Standing Bear, chief of the Ponca tribe, lost both his son and his daughter. His son's dying wish was to be buried in his homeland. Chief Standing Bear promised to do this and kept his promise. When he and thirty of his fellow tribesmen returned to Nebraska, however, they were thrown into prison.

U.S. Army General George Crook, one of Abraham Lincoln's former Boys in Blue, realized this was wrong. It is believed that he alerted a reporter of the *Omaha Daily-Herald*. Thomas Tibbles, the reporter, wrote about this terrible injustice, and the news spread throughout America. Chief Standing Bear sued the U.S. government for imprisoning him and his clansmen. Judge Elmer Dundy presided over the trial. In an amazing coincidence, Abraham Lincoln himself had appointed Elmer Dundy to the position of U.S. judge.

During the suspense-filled trial Chief Standing Bear pleaded:

> *This hand is not the same color as yours but if I pierce it, I shall feel pain. The blood that will flow from mine will be the same color as yours. I am a man. The same God made us both.*

Judge Dundy agreed. He ruled Standing Bear and his immediate band were "persons" under U.S. law and could sue for their freedom. He then set Standing Bear and his Ponca tribesmen free. Abraham Lincoln, who had always treated Native Americans with respect, would have been proud of these Americans who stood for what is right.

"[Thou shalt] love thy neighbour as thyself."

—MATTHEW 22:39 (KJV), quoted by Abraham Lincoln

Chief Standing Bear boldly dressed in full Native American regalia for his trial.

Anderson with Union veterans from Hemingford in Box Butte County.

LIKE ABRAHAM LINCOLN, former slave Robert Ball Anderson lived an exemplary life. Anderson grew up in Kentucky, just two counties away from Lincoln's birthplace. The wife of Anderson's master was cruel and Anderson's entire body became scarred from her punishments. After one whipping she tortured him further by rubbing pepper into his wounds and soaking him in brine. Finally, Anderson escaped, enlisted in the Union Army, and mustered into the 125th Colored Infantry. "All of us were anxious to get into the fray," he explained, but the war ended before he saw action. He was then dispatched to the western front to fight Native American Indians as a "buffalo soldier." (Indians gave this name to black troops, perhaps because of their skin color.) A man of integrity and compassion, Anderson endured the wrath of his commander when he defied an order to shoot an Indian woman and her baby. While out West, Anderson boldly began to dream of owning his own land.

Anderson moved to Nebraska's Box Butte County in 1884 to homestead. Ever honest and frugal, he steadily expanded his farm. Recruiting black youths as his hired hands, he admonished them to live in such a way that all would say, "It [the Civil War] was, indeed, a glorious victory." With deep appreciation he said, "All honor and glory to those who laid down their lives that the black man might be free." Referring to the Bible, he added, "Surely 'greater love hath no man than this, that he lay down his life' for the freedom of a race."

By the late 1800s, Robert Ball Anderson had acquired more than two thousand acres to become the largest black landowner in Nebraska. Describing his fellow Nebraskans, he said, "I cannot help but feel that everyone in Box Butte County and western Nebraska, regardless of color, is my friend and I am proud of it." Anderson elaborated, "I find that there is no greater rule for making and holding friends, for happiness and contentment and real enjoyment of life, than in doing unto others as I would like them to do unto me, and try to do it just a little bit better." Thus, thanks to Abraham Lincoln, the Boys in Blue, and his own perseverance and integrity, Anderson was able to realize his daring dream.

Robert Ball Anderson in 1927.

"The fear of the Lord is the beginning of wisdom."
—PSALM 111:10 (KJV), quoted by Abraham Lincoln

Children from an orphan train line up at a local train station so that prospective parents could choose which child or children to adopt.

As the 1800s drew to a close, Nebraskans began welcoming children from orphan trains. These trains carried street children from the slums of New York City mainly to families in the Midwest and West. Some children were orphans, but others were from families who simply could not afford to feed them.

Reverend Swan of Nebraska joined this effort as an agent. In this position he chaperoned children, helped to find them homes, then visited them regularly. Agents also tried to ensure that children were not being used as laborers. Children loved Reverend Swan so much that they called him "Grandpa," or even "Sweet Grandpa Swan."

Mr. and Mrs. Carman from McCook, Nebraska, welcomed a street child named Claretta Brown into their home. Claretta later explained:

I was a lost and lonely child, just eight years old, not very well, and a long way from home. . . . When I was put to bed that [first] night . . . I cried my heart out. It had been long overdue. Mrs. Carman never had any children of her own and had a heart as big as all outdoors. She stayed with me until the tears were over and I at last fell asleep. The next morning things looked a lot brighter. It took me a year with 'tender loving care' to get going again.

For almost forty years the orphan trains stopped at towns throughout the state. Nebraska families welcomed more than six thousand street children into their homes and showed them love.

"I shall be most happy indeed if I shall be an humble instrument in the hands of the Almighty."
—Abraham Lincoln

Father Flanagan, pictured here at the second, larger home in Omaha.

OMAHA, NEBRASKA, BEGAN TO STRUGGLE WITH numerous street children of its own during World War I. Father Edward Flanagan, a priest in Omaha, decided to help by welcoming five children into a former boarding house he had rented. Soon, he had twenty boys and not enough food or beds. When they received a barrel of sauerkraut, it was the only food they had to eat for their first Christmas dinner. In a short time, Father Flanagan had one hundred boys in his home. There certainly were not enough beds for so many boys. Father Flanagan placed straw bedding inside chicken coops, then stacked the chicken coops like bunk beds. There may not have been enough proper beds for so many boys, but the home overflowed with love.

One of the many homeless boys in Omaha.

When Nebraskans learned about Father Flanagan's efforts, they began to contribute money and gifts. The boys were then moved to a larger home. Eventually they outgrew this home and moved to a farm. The farm bustled with classrooms, small trade schools for the boys, chores to be done, and athletic activities. Eventually, Boys Town began grouping the boys into "families" on the campus. This group home approach proved effective and spread across the United States.

In 1979 it added a program for girls. Eventually it became a national research center on learning disabilities, as another way to help troubled youths. Its counseling services have ministered to hundreds of thousands of hurting families. To this day, Boys Town continues to follow Abraham Lincoln's "bright example" of doing what is right.

> "So far as able, within my sphere, I have always acted as I believed to be right and just; and I have done all I could for the good of mankind."
> —ABRAHAM LINCOLN

Edward Parsons Smith was described as "one of the bravest and best men."

"The judgments of the Lord are righteous and true altogether."

—Psalm 19:9 (kjv), quoted by Abraham Lincoln

THE KINDNESS OF FATHER FLANAGAN WAS IN STARK contrast to the evil that characterized Omaha in the early 1900s. Indeed, Omaha's political boss Tom Dennison oversaw profligate crime and prostitution. In 1919 Edward Parsons Smith stepped forward to campaign in the mayoral election on a reform platform. Backed by the Omaha Church Federation, Smith won and began to take on the Dennison machine. Dennison retaliated, however, by fomenting racial unrest. The ensuing tension exploded when police arrested Will Brown, a black man, for assaulting a white woman. This charge was never substantiated.

Inflamed by Dennison backers, thousands gathered around the courthouse that housed the jail. Chanting "Lynch him! Lynch him!" they demanded Will Brown's release. Inside, Mayor Smith and the sheriff vainly sought reinforcements. Suddenly, Edward Smith did the unthinkable. He unlocked the courthouse door, walked outside, and faced the rioters. As ringleaders placed a noose around his neck he said, "If you must lynch someone, let it be me." They proceeded to hang him and then stormed the courthouse. In the chaos, city detectives raced to retrieve the mayor's body. They discovered Smith was still alive and rushed him to a hospital. Meanwhile, the mob celebrated wildly after killing Will Brown. At long last, federal troops arrived to restore order.

Smith struggled to survive and deliriously repeated, "They cannot get him," and "Mob rule will not prevail in Omaha." Miraculously, the mayor recovered and served out his term, but he was unable to implement further reform. In 1932 the federal government indicted Dennison on conspiracy charges and broke the machine's stranglehold on Omaha.

This riot was the lowest point in Nebraska's history as a state. Yet in the midst of the depravity, Edward Parsons Smith stood for right and was willing to lay down his life for another. In so doing, he emulated Abraham Lincoln's beautiful example.

Mob leaders climb the courthouse to capture their victim.

In 1920 more than a million children between 10 and 15 years of age worked in factories and mines, often using machines manufactured specifically for child laborers.

Grace Abbott and Abraham Lincoln shared a selfless determination to help the oppressed. Indeed, Abbott impacted the lives of millions of immigrants and also became one of our country's greatest crusaders for children's rights.

Abbott was born in 1878 in Grand Island. Grace's father had served as one of Lincoln's Boys in Blue and her mother campaigned vigorously for women's suffrage. At an age when few women attended college, Abbott graduated from Grand Island College and obtained master's degrees from the University of Nebraska and the University of Chicago.

In Chicago, as the director of the Immigrants' Protective League, she fought for the rights of immigrants. In 1921 she was appointed to the headship of the Children's Bureau in the U.S. Department of Labor. During her thirteen-year tenure, Abbott tirelessly led the battle to abolish child labor in this country. Because of the high U.S. infant mortality rate, she also advanced maternal and child healthcare. She even addressed juvenile delinquency and human trafficking.

Abbott explained that some people ask: "Why should anyone . . . seek a part in the struggle to end the injustice and ugliness of our modern life?" Referring to *Pilgrim's Progress*, she continued, "They are the lotus-eaters who prefer to live in a gray twilight in which there is neither victory nor defeat. It is impossible for them to understand that to have had a part in the struggle, to have done what one could, is in itself the reward of effort and the comfort in defeat." She died in 1939, a champion for those in need.

"Let us diligently apply the means, never doubting that a just God, in his own good time, will give us the rightful result."

—Abraham Lincoln

> "Eternal right makes might—as we understand our duty, let us do it!"
>
> —ABRAHAM LINCOLN

Another equally remarkable story began with the outbreak of World War II. At that time, U.S. soldiers traveled on trains that still followed the route of the transcontinental railroad through Nebraska. These "troop trains" all stopped briefly at the train station in North Platte, in western Nebraska. (North Platte just happens to be in Lincoln County.)

When the war began, North Platte citizens heard that a train carrying "their boys" would be coming through. Five hundred townspeople arrived bearing food and gifts. When they boarded the train, they discovered the soldiers were actually from Kansas. They gave their gifts to these appreciative soldiers. Afterwards, a young woman named Rae Wilson wrote to the local paper. She suggested that the town turn its railroad station into a canteen (a citizen-run restaurant for soldiers). That way they could welcome any soldiers who stopped at their train station.

The town rallied behind her idea. On Christmas Day in 1941 they launched the North Platte Canteen. Day and night, for more than four years, townspeople prepared and served bottles of milk, sandwiches, pies, and cakes—even birthday cakes—to U.S. troops. Because the U.S. government strictly limited food supplies, North Platte citizens had to be resourceful. For instance, they often used pheasant meat in the sandwiches and turkey eggs in the cakes. A total of fifty-five thousand volunteers worked at the Canteen. These included young people and at least one mother who had lost her own son in the war. People from western Nebraska all the way to eastern Colorado also donated food and money to help the effort. Many volunteers would have agreed with one woman's description that "you would feel like you had done something worthwhile, for the glory of God and the glory of your nation." By war's end, they had served six million soldiers. These U.S. soldiers especially treasured the love that had been shown to them—the real kind of love.

ABOVE: Platform volunteers from the North Platte Canteen greet a troop train.

RIGHT: (from left) Rae Wilson, Edwina Barraclough and Katie Foust greeted servicemen during the early days of the Canteen.

S TILL TODAY, THE MEMBERS OF THE U.S. MILITARY FOLLOW Abraham Lincoln's shining example. The courageous and selfless actions of Nebraska's Private First Class Edward Gomez illustrate this. Born in Omaha in 1932, his father worked at a meatpacking plant while his mother cared for their twelve children. Edward, their third child, did well at school and even became a Golden Glove featherweight boxer. His brothers and sisters appreciated how he protected them against neighborhood bullies.

In 1949, at the age of seventeen, he convinced his father to allow him to enlist in the Marine Corps Reserve. A year later, the Korean War began and Private Gomez was called up and shipped to Pusan, Korea. Immediately, he was flown fifty miles behind the lines to fight as a machine-gunner with "Easy" Company, Second Battalion, First Marine Regiment.

Wounded in the leg, Gomez received a Purple Heart and soon returned to the field. Just one month after his nineteenth birthday, his machine gun squad advanced in a bold assault. During a nighttime lull in the fierce fight, Gomez presciently wrote to his family, "I'm writing this letter on the possibility that I may die in this next assault." He explained that he was willing to do this for his country and then directed his thoughts to his younger brothers and sisters. "Kids, fight only for what you believe in," he wrote from his foxhole. "That's what I'm fighting for."

At dawn the firefight resumed. Suddenly, a hostile grenade landed in their trench. Oscar Franco, his good friend and fellow soldier, recounted that in a split-second Gomez picked it up, spun his body away from them, and fell on the grenade to absorb the explosion. "He saved my life," Franco recalled with deep emotion. Gomez was awarded the Medal of Honor—the highest military decoration for valor—for "conspicuous gallantry and intrepidity at the risk of his life and beyond the call of duty." Indeed, Edward Gomez made the ultimate sacrifice to save his buddies and willingly gave his life for the country that he loved.

Private First Class Edward Gomez received a Medal of Honor, the highest military decoration for valor.

> "I have said nothing but what I am willing to live by and, in the pleasure of Almighty God, die by."
> —ABRAHAM LINCOLN

These select stories illustrate how Nebraskans have emulated Abraham Lincoln's way of living. As Nebraskans have done this, his capital star has shown brilliantly thoughout the state. But is the Lincoln star shining brightly today? Are its beams radiating not only throughout Nebraska, but also throughout our country? That depends on whether each one of us will try our best to imitate Abraham Lincoln's excellent ways.

Remember that the first step is to promise with determination to follow Abraham Lincoln's example. Recall that with a character of love, he aimed to be right and do right. How can we know what is right? According to Abraham Lincoln himself, the only way to know right from wrong is to know the Bible. What was the secret of Abraham Lincoln's success? Reverend Gurley said it was Lincoln's abiding confidence in God and Lincoln's belief that truth and righteousness would triumph through God and for God's glory.

Here are a few of the countless ways in which we can live as Abraham Lincoln did:

- In trying situations, we can recognize what is wrong and do what is right.
- We can befriend those who are in need, whether in our neighborhood, in our workplace, or perhaps even in a nursing home.
- We can do our part to help relieve the suffering of the poor and the oppressed.

Every day we will have new opportunities to do what is right. Sometimes we will even be able to work together to carry this out. Both individually and collectively, this can become our way of living.

How amazed Abraham Lincoln would have been to learn that out West, in the prairie that he loved, a state capital is named in his honor. He would be especially delighted to learn that this capital star is in the state of Nebraska. Perhaps he would remember how the Nebraska Bill actually set him on the path to the presidency. He would have been pleased to learn that his presidential decisions expertly guided the growth of Nebraska and its capital city.

Abraham Lincoln would have been both encouraged and humbled to learn that his capital star still shines as Nebraskans follow his example. How Abraham Lincoln would want each Nebraskan to depend on God to know and pursue what is right. How he would hope that this would be true not just throughout Nebraska but also throughout the entire United States that he so loved.

After Lincoln's death, Dr. C.N. Hoffman eloquently predicted that "the golden rays of his [Abraham Lincoln's] 'bright example' shall long continue to . . . [illuminate] the hilltops and valleys of our entire land." This will only happen if we each promise—right now and with determination—to emulate Lincoln's bright example. Indeed, this would be the truest mark of our respect and the best tribute we could ever offer Abraham Lincoln.

> "The golden rays of his [Abraham Lincoln's] bright example shall long continue to . . . [illuminate] the hill tops and valleys of our entire land."
>
> —C.N. Hoffman, M.D.
> May 30, 1865

PERHAPS, JUST PERHAPS, if Abraham Lincoln could have heard this story, he would have responded with a letter like this:

My Dear Friends,

    I cannot wait to tell Mary and our boys about the Lincoln capital star. Of course, they will want to start packing their bags so that we can immediately travel by rail to visit the beautiful state of Nebraska. I can just imagine Tad and Willie racing up the steps of the Nebraska state capitol to get a bird's-eye view of the city named Lincoln. It will be a thrilling trip.

    It is humbling to think that my life has been called a "bright example." Always, I simply tried to know and to do what is right. As I've often written, I depended on God to do this. I believe that, with God's help, you can do this, too. I look forward to learning about the countless, unique ways in which Nebraskans will live this out. I hope that more and more Americans will recognize and do what is right, so that our country will remain united and great. That will be the finest tribute of all.

                        Respectfully yours,

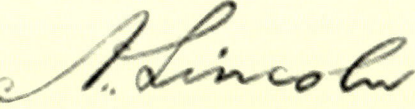

SELECTED BIBLIOGRAPHY

Abraham Lincoln's Classroom, The Lincoln Institute and The Lehrman Institute. Web. Multiple times. 2005-2009. <http://www.abrahamlincolnsclassroom.org>.

Abraham Lincoln Online. Abraham Lincoln Online.org. Web. Multiple times. 2005-2009. <http://showcase.netins.net/web/creative/lincoln.html>.

Ambrose, Stephen E. *Undaunted Courage*. New York: Simon & Schuster, 1996. Print.

Bell, Blake. Historian, Homestead National Monument of America. Personal and e-mail interviews. 2010.

Bergh, Albert Ellery, and Richard Holland Johnston, eds. *The Writings of Thomas Jefferson*. Virginia: Thomas Jefferson Memorial Association, Volume 16. Google Books. Web. June, 2009.

Boritt, Gabor. *The Gettysburg Gospel*. New York: Simon & Schuster, 2006. Print.

Bromley, John. Director of Historic Programs, Union Pacific Railroad. Personal and e-mail interviews. 2010.

Cornelius, James M. Curator, Abraham Lincoln Presidential Library & Museum. Personal and e-mail interviews. 2008-2009.

Federer, William J. *America's God and Country*. Coppell, Texas: FAME, 1994. Print.

Fitzpatrick, Lilian Linder. "Nebraska Place-names." University of Nebraska Studies in Language, Literature, and Criticism, No. 6, 1925. NEGenWeb Project Online Library Presentation. Web. Sept. 21, 2007. <http://digitalcommons.unl.edu/englishunsllc/1/>.

Gomez, Modesto. Brother of Edward Gomez. Phone interview. January 21, 2010.

Goodwin, Doris Kearns. *Team of Rivals*. New York: Simon & Schuster, 2005. Print.

Greene, Bob. *Once Upon a Town: The Miracle of the North Platte Canteen*. New York: William Morrow, 2002. Print.

Huffman, Wendell. Curator of History, Nevada State Railroad Museum. Personal interview. 2010.

Kent, Emerson. "History for the Relaxed Historian." Web. Multiple times. 2008-2010. <http://ww.emerson-kent.com>.

Leonard, Daisy Anderson. *From Slavery to Affluence: Memoirs of Robert Anderson, Ex-Slave*. Colorado: Steamboat Springs Pilot, 1927. Print.

Lubin, Martin, ed. *The Words of Abraham Lincoln*. New York: Black Dog & Leventhal, 2005. Print.

Lynch, Tom. Hall of History Director, Boys Town. E-mail interviews. 2009.

Martens, Gary. "Seward County, Nebraska." American Local History Project, 1999. Web. Sept. 10, 2008. <http://seward.wathenadesigns.com>.

McKee, James L. *Lincoln: The Prairie Capital*. Lincoln, Nebraska: J&L Lee Publishers. Print.

Medal of Honor, U.S. Army Center of Military History. Web. January 14, 2010. <http://www.history.army.mil/html/moh/koreanwar.html>.

The New Chain–Reference Bible, King James Version. Frank C. Thompson. Indianapolis, Indiana: B. B. Kirkbride Bible. 1964. Print.

Olson, James C., and Ronald C. Naugle. *History of Nebraska*. Lincoln, Nebraska: University of Nebraska Press, 1997. Print.

Omaha's Riot in Story and Picture, 1919. The Educational Publishing Company. Web. January 8, 2010. <histori-comaha.com/riot>.

Patrick, Michael, Evelyn Sheets, and Evelyn Trickel. *We Are a Part of History: The Story of the Orphan Train*. Santa Fe, New Mexico: Lightning Tree, 1991. Print.

Potter, James E. Senior Research Historian, Nebraska Historical Society. Personal and e-mail interviews. 2008-2009.

Potter, James E., and Edith Robbins, eds. *Marching With the First Nebraska, A Civil War Diary, by August Scherneckau*. Norman: University of Oklahoma Press, 2007. Print.

Potts, James B. "North of 'Bleeding Kansas': The 1850s Political Crisis in Nebraska Territory." *Nebraska History*, Fall (1992): 110-117. Print.

Taylor, Quintard. *In Search of the Racial Frontier: African Americans in the West,* 1528-1990. New York: W.W. Norton and Company, 1998. Print.

Robinette, Gary. Culture Director, Ponca Tribe of Nebraska. E-mail interview. March 26, 2009.

Rosenberg, Gary R. Research Specialist, Douglas County Historical Society. E-mail interviews. 2010.

Smith, Jeffrey H., and Phillip Thomas Tucker, eds. *The 1862 Plot to Kidnap Jefferson Davis, by Victor Vifquain*. Mechanicsburg, PA: Stackpole Books, 1998. Print.

Sorenson, John. Director of the Abbott Sisters Project. E-mail interviews. 2010.

Sorenson, John, with Judith Sealander, eds. *The Grace Abbott Reader.* Lincoln, Nebraska: University of Nebraska Press, 2008. Print.

Starita, Joe. *I Am a Man.* New York: St. Martin's, 2008. Print.

State Council of Pennsylvania. *In Memoriam: Abraham Lincoln, President of the United States.* Philadelphia: Geo. Hawkes, Jr., 1865. Google Books. Web. Jan 24, 2009.

Stroble, Paul E. "The Vandalia Statehouse and the Relocation to Springfield." Illinois Periodicals Online Project of the Northern Illinois University Libraries. Web. September, 2009. www.lib.niu.edu/2000/ihsp0012.html.

Thomas, Benjamin P. *Abraham Lincoln.* New York: Barnes & Noble Books, 1994. Print.

PICTURE CREDITS

ILLUSTRATIONS

Pages 7, 8, 10, 19, 23, and 24 by Carol Tornatore of Nokomis, Florida.

Maps created by Pete Chadwell of Bend, Oregon

Maps based in part on maps compiled by H. George Stoll, Hammond, Inc., 1967; revised by U.S. Geological Survey, 1970.

COVER

Skyscape: © Winston Barclay of Iowa City, Iowa, donated this photograph entitled "Prairie Sun." It was taken in the Nebraska Northwest Panhandle.

Landscape: © Paul Johnsgard of Lincoln, Nebraska, donated this tallgrass prairie photo.

Abraham Lincoln: © Ron Coddington of Arlington, Virginia, colorized and donated this image. It is based on a photograph by Alexander Gardner, courtesy of the Library of Congress, (Digital File Number: cph.3a53289).

Campaign button courtesy of the Hudson Library and Historical Society in Hudson, Ohio.

Page 1: © Gary Tonhouse of Ankeny, Iowa, donated this tallgrass prairie photograph. His images are found at www.reflectiveimages.com.

Pages 2, 3: © Paul Johnsgard donated this tallgrass prairie photograph.

Page 4: Photograph by Anthony Berger courtesy of the Library of Congress, Prints and Photographs Division, (LC-USZC4-2777).

Page 7: Observatory photograph (10c) courtesy of the U.S. Naval Observatory Library.

Page 9: © Garry Rose of Rose Photography in O'Fallon, Missouri, donated this photograph of Lewis and Clark. Pat Kennedy is the sculptor.

Page 10: © Raymond Bial of Urbana, Illinois, donated this photograph of Abraham Lincoln's birthplace. His images and books are found at www.raybial.com.

Page 11: © Jurgen Brauer of Augusta, Georgia, donated this photograph of the wilderness.

Page 12: © Justin Reed of Lincoln, Nebraska, donated this photograph entitled "Gifts from the Prairie." His images are found at www.CopperCreekImages.com.

Page 13: Kevin Dier-Zimmel of Beaver Dam, Wisconsin, contributed this slave advertisement from *The Washington Globe*, Washington City, February 23, 1837. (This image is found at the abolition Web site: www.wlhn.org/topics/abolition.)

Slave pen photograph courtesy of the National Archives, (Identifier 530504).

Pages 14, 15: © Phyllis Reagan of Lincoln, Nebraska, donated this tallgrass prairie photograph.

Page 15: © David Blanchette of the Illinois Historic Preservation Agency donated this photograph of Fred M. Torrey's sculpture entitled "Lincoln the Circuit Rider."

Page 16: Image courtesy of the National Archives, (Identifier 528297/Local Identifier 111-B-4151).

Page 17: Photograph by Samuel Alschuler courtesy of the Library of Congress, Rare Book and Special Collections Division, (lprbscsm scsm1050).

Page 20: Abraham Lincoln and Hannibal Hamlin lithograph courtesy of the Library of Congress, Prints and Photographs Division, (LC-USZC4-7996).

Knox College of Galesburg, Illinois, donated this painting by Victor Perard.

Page 21: Painting by Jean Louis Gerome Ferris in 1908, courtesy of the Library of Congress, Prints and Photographs Division, (LC-cph-3g-10753).

Page 22: U.S. Capitol photograph courtesy of the Library of Congress, Prints and Photographs Division, (LC-USZ62-75795).

Page 25: The Strobridge Lith. Co., Cincinnati, image entitled "Abraham Lincoln and His Emancipation Proclamation," courtesy of the Library of Congress, Prints and Photographs Division, (LC-USZC4-1526).

Page 26: © Phyllis Reagan donated this saltgrass photograph.

Page 27: Photograph by Andrew Gardner courtesy of the Library of Congress, Prints and Photographs Division, (LC-DIG-ppmsca-19191).

Page 28: Photograph of prairie sunset donated by © Eric W. Valentine, www.praisephotography.com.

Photograph of the Oak Creek Cemetery receiving vault courtesy of the Abraham Lincoln Presidential Library & Museum (ALPLM).

Page 29: Alvin Saunders image courtesy of the Library of Congress, Prints and Photographs Division, (LC-DIG-cwpbh-03922).

The Homestead National Monument of America donated this photograph of men plowing.

Page 30: The Homestead National Monument of America donated these two photographs of homesteaders.

Page 31: The Union Pacific Museum donated this photograph taken by John Carbutt in October 1866.

Page 32: Battle of Fort Donelson image courtesy of the Library of Congress, Prints and Photographs Division, (LC-DIG-pga-01849).

Battle of Shiloh image courtesy of the Library of Congress, Prints and Photographs Division, (LC-USZC2-3769).

Page 33: Image courtesy of the Nebraska State Historical Society, (RG4389-19).

Page 34: Image courtesy of the Nebraska State Historical Society, (RG2608-1784).

Page 35: Image courtesy of the Nebraska State Historical Society, (RG1792:6-4).

Page 36: The Great Seal of the State of Nebraska is used with the permission of the Nebraska Secretary of State.

Page 37: Lancaster Village photograph courtesy of the Nebraska State Historical Society, (RG2158-38a).

Photograph of the first Nebraska Capitol courtesy of the Nebraska State Historical Society, (RG1234-16).

Page 38: Clay, Henry—Kentuckian orator and statesman whom Lincoln respected. Image courtesy of the National Archives, (ARC Identifier 528344).

Colfax, Schuyler—Republican congressman. Image courtesy of the Library of Congress, Prints and Photographs Division, (LC-DIG-cwpb-01935).

Custer, George A.—Civil War major general. Image courtesy of the Library of Congress, Prints and Photographs Division, (LC-DIG-cwpb-03216).

Douglas, Stephen A.—Image courtesy of the National Archives, (ARC Identifier 52829).

Dundy, Elmer S.— Judge appointed by Abraham Lincoln in 1863 to associate justice of the Supreme Court of the Nebraska Territory for the area south of the Platte River. Image courtesy of the Nebraska State Historical Society, (RG2411-1422).

Furnas, Robert W.—Civil War colonel, Second Nebraska Cavalry. Image courtesy of the Nebraska State Historical Society, (RG4389-2).

Garfield, James A.—Twentieth president and Civil War major general. Image courtesy of the Library of Congress, Prints and Photographs Division, (LC-DIG-cwpb-06455).

Grant, Ulysses S.—Civil War general-in-chief. Image courtesy of the Library of Congress, Prints and Photographs Division, (LC-DIG-cwpb-06947).

Greeley, Horace—News editor and abolitionist. Image courtesy of the Library of Congress, Prints and Photographs Division, Hoxie Collection, (LC-DIG-cwpbh-00704).

Hayes, Rutherford B.—Nineteenth president and Civil War major general. Image courtesy of the Library of Congress, Prints and Photographs Division, (LCDIG-cwpbh-03606).

Holt, Joseph—Civil War brigadier general. Image courtesy of the Library of Congress, Prints and Photographs Division, (LC-DIG-cwpb-06703).

Hooker, Joseph—Civil War major general. Image courtesy of the Library of Congress, Prints and Photographs Division, (LC-DIG-cwpb-06979).

Howard, Oliver O.—Civil War general. Image courtesy of the Library of Congress, Prints and Photographs Division, (LC-DIG-cwpb-06599).

Logan, John A.—Civil War major general. Image courtesy of the Library of Congress, Prints and Photographs Division, (LC-DIG-cwpb-07018).

McPherson, James B.—Civil War major general. Image courtesy of the Library of Congress, Prints and Photographs Division, (LC-DIG-cwpb-07051).

Saunders, Alvin E.—Nebraska territorial governor appointed by Abraham Lincoln. Image courtesy of the Library of Congress, Prints and Photographs Division, (LC-DIG-cwpbh-03922).

Seward, William H.—Lincoln's secretary of state. Image courtesy of the Library of Congress, Prints and Photographs Division, (LC-DIG-cph-3a23003).

Sheridan, Phillip H.—Civil War major general. Image courtesy of the National Archives, (ARC Identifier: 526708).

Sherman, William T.—Civil War major general. Image courtesy of the Library of Congress, Prints and Photographs Division, (LC-DIG-cwpb-07136).

Stanton, Edwin M.—Lincoln's secretary of war. Image courtesy of the Library of Congress, Prints and Photographs Division, Brady-Handy Collection, (LC-DIG-cwpbh-00960).

Thayer, John M.—Nebraskan and Civil War major general. Image courtesy of the Nebraska State Historical Society, (RG2720-1a).

Thomas, George H.—Civil War major general. Image courtesy of the Library of Congress, Prints and Photographs Division, (LC-DIG-cwpbh-01069).

Webster, Daniel—Orator and statesman whom Abraham Lincoln respected. Image courtesy of the National Archives, (ARC Identifier: 528348).

Page 39: © Lincoln Chamber of Commerce, Lincoln, Nebraska, donated this photograph of the Nebraska Capitol.

Page 40: Photograph by Alexander Gardner on April 10, 1865, courtesy of the Library of Congress, (Digital File Number: cph.3a53289).

Page 41: Image courtesy of the Nebraska State Historical Society, (RG2858-1).

Page 42: Image courtesy of the Nebraska State Historical Society, (RG1227:2-2).

Page 43: Union veterans photograph courtesy of the Nebraska State Historical Society, (RG2301:6-21).

Robert Ball Anderson photograph courtesy of the Nebraska State Historical Society, (RG2973:2-2.)

Page 44: The © Patrick-Sheets-Trickel Collection in Trenton, Missouri, donated these two images.

Page 45: The © Boys Town Hall of History Museum donated the photograph of Father Flanagan, and the photograph by Bostwick of a homeless boy.

Page 46: Image of Edward Parsons Smith donated by the Douglas County Historical Society; artist is Werthman Constable.

Courthouse photograph courtesy of the Nebraska State Historical Society. (RG2467:0-6).

Page 47: Photograph of Grace Abbott donated by the Stuhr Museum of the Prairie Pioneer.

Photograph of the child laborer courtesy of the Library of Congress, Prints and Photographs Division, (LC-DIG-nclc-01357).

Page 48: The © Union Pacific Museum donated these photographs of the North Platte Canteen.

Page 49: © Kevin C. Radik of Omaha, Nebraska, donated the gravesite image.

© Crystal Gomez Keele-Zimmermann of Omaha, Nebraska, donated this photograph of a painting of Edward Gomez. Artist unknown.

Page 50: © David Dale of David Dale Photography (www.daviddalephoto.com) in Lincoln, Nebraska, donated this photograph of the Abraham Lincoln statue at the Nebraska Capitol. Sculptor is Daniel Chester French.

Page 51: © Gary Friedman of Huntington Beach, California (FriedmanArchives.com) donated this photograph of the Lincoln Memorial in Washington, D.C. Sculptor is Daniel Chester French.

Page 52: TOP: © Stephen Weaver of Colorado Springs, Colorado (www.stephenweaver.com), donated this photograph entitled "Nebraska Prairie Sunset" taken near Valentine, Nebraska.

©Terrell Creative, Inc., of Kansas City, Missouri (www.terrellcreative.com) donated the photograph of Lincoln, Nebraska.

John Carrel of Beatrice, Nebraska, donated the photograph of the Nebraska Capitol.

The Great Seal of the State of Nebraska used with the permission of the Nebraska Secretary of State.

The Nebraska quarter-dollar image courtesy of the United States Mint.

Bottom: ©Paul Johnsgard donated this prairie photograph.

Page 53: Allison Dittman of Lincoln, Nebraska, illustrated Abraham Lincoln's hat.

ACKNOWLEDGMENTS

This book represents several years of sleuthing and rewriting to arrive at a historically accurate story. It was an amazing journey, especially because of the kindness shown to me along the way.

My husband, John, and our four children endured the early drafts with humor and steadfast encouragement. Eleanor Gillett, Ellen Kohl, Carolyn Kroeker, Roberta Newburn, and Barb Wallingford provided invaluable direction. And a special thank you to Michelle Nash who volunteered as editor.

Dr. James M. Cornelius, Curator of the Abraham Lincoln Presidential Library & Museum, and James E. Potter, Senior Research Historian of the Nebraska State Historical Society, patiently spent hours to ensure historical accuracy.

Blake Bell, Historian of the Homestead National Monument of America, and John Bromley, Director of Historic Programs for the Union Pacific Railroad, also lent their expertise. So did Wendell Huffman, Curator of History of the Nevada State Railroad Museum, Tom Lynch, Hall of History Director at Boys Town, Gary Robinette, Culture Director of the Ponca Tribe of Nebraska, Gary Rosenberg, Research Specialist at the Douglas County Historical Society, prairie expert Ernest Rousek, and John Sorenson, Director of the Abbott Sisters Project.

Abraham Lincoln impersonator Lee Williams and commercial photographer Don Farrell collaborated for a Lincoln model for illustrations.

The following regionally and nationally recognized photographers donated images:

- Raymond Bial
- David Dale
- Gary Friedman
- Paul Johnsgard
- Garry Rose
- Gary Tonhouse
- Eric W. Valentine
- Stephen Weaver

In addition, these amateur photographers donated stunning photos: Winston Barclay, David Blanchette, Jurgen Brauer, John Carrel, Ron Coddington, Crystal Keele-Zimmermann, Kevin Radik, Phyllis Reagan, and Justin Reed. The Nebraska Secretary of State and the Lincoln Chamber of Commerce shared images. The Boys Town Hall of History, the Homestead National Monument of America, the Patrick-Sheets-Trickel Collection, the Stuhr Museum of the Prairie Pioneer, and the Union Pacific Museum also donated photographs. So did Terrell Creative, Inc., the Douglas County Historical Society, Knox College, the Hudson Library and Historical Society, and Kevin Dier-Zimmel. Kasey Moon helped prepare the maps for Pete Chadwell.

This book would not be possible without the support of many, including Becca and Geoff Basler, Alice Dittman, Don and Julie Henslee, Mike and Kim Marsh, Mary-Jo Miller, Susan Napolitano, Mary Perini, Bill and Grace Scanlan, and Tom Scanlan. Thank you, also, to the teachers who reviewed the manuscript, including Patsy Bruner and Theresa Reinhard. Finally, it was a delight to work with book designer Carol Tornatore.

Together, we did it! May our efforts inspire many to emulate Abraham Lincoln's bright example.

All proceeds from the sale of this book will be donated to Great Kids Helping Great Kids, Inc., a storytelling ministry in Lincoln, Nebraska.

Copyright © 2010 by Susan Grace Dittman

All rights reserved, including the right to reproduce this book or portions thereof in any form whatsoever.

2009913667
Library of Congress Cataloging-in-Publication Data has been applied for.
ISBN-13: 978-0-615-34265-8

Illustrations by Carol Tornatore

Maps © 2010 by Pete Chadwell

First hardcover edition October, 2010

Manufactured in the United States of America.